ROUTLEDGE LIBRARY EDITIONS:
LIBRARY AND INFORMATION SCIENCE

Volume 27

DEVELOPING LIBRARY STAFF FOR THE 21ST CENTURY

DEVELOPING LIBRARY STAFF FOR THE 21ST CENTURY

Edited by
MAUREEN SULLIVAN

LONDON AND NEW YORK

First published in 1992 by The Haworth Press, Inc.

This edition first published in 2020
by Routledge
2 Park Square, Milton Park, Abingdon, Oxon OX14 4RN

and by Routledge
52 Vanderbilt Avenue, New York, NY 10017

Routledge is an imprint of the Taylor & Francis Group, an informa business

© 1992 The Haworth Press, Inc.

All rights reserved. No part of this book may be reprinted or reproduced or utilised in any form or by any electronic, mechanical, or other means, now known or hereafter invented, including photocopying and recording, or in any information storage or retrieval system, without permission in writing from the publishers.

Trademark notice: Product or corporate names may be trademarks or registered trademarks, and are used only for identification and explanation without intent to infringe.

British Library Cataloguing in Publication Data
A catalogue record for this book is available from the British Library

ISBN: 978-0-367-34616-4 (Set)
ISBN: 978-0-429-34352-0 (Set) (ebk)
ISBN: 978-0-367-40458-1 (Volume 27) (hbk)
ISBN: 978-0-367-40459-8 (Volume 27) (pbk)
ISBN: 978-0-429-35625-4 (Volume 27) (ebk)

Publisher's Note
The publisher has gone to great lengths to ensure the quality of this reprint but points out that some imperfections in the original copies may be apparent.

Disclaimer
The publisher has made every effort to trace copyright holders and would welcome correspondence from those they have been unable to trace.

Developing Library Staff for the 21st Century

Maureen Sullivan
Editor

The Haworth Press, Inc.
New York • London • Norwood(Australia)

Developing Library Staff for the 21st Century has also been published as *Journal of Library Administration*, Volume 17, Number 1 1992.

© 1992 by The Haworth Press, Inc. All rights reserved. No part of this work may be reproduced or utilized in any form or by any means, electronic or mechanical, including photocopying, microfilm and recording, or by any information storage and retrieval system, without permission in writing from the publisher. Printed in the United States of America.

Paperback edition published in 1996.

The Haworth Press, Inc., 10 Alice Street, Binghamton, NY 13904-1580 USA

Library of Congress Cataloging-in-Publication Data

Developing library staff for the 21st century / Maureen Sullivan, editor.
    p. cm.
Includes bibliographical references.
ISBN 0-7890-0067-9
  1. Library personnel management–United States. I. Sullivan, Maureen.
Z682.2.U5D48 1992
023'.9–dc20   92-27399
                                                                                                            CIP

Developing Library Staff for the 21st Century

CONTENTS

Introduction *Maureen Sullivan*	1
Preparing Academic and Research Library Staff for the 1990's and Beyond *Susan Jurow*	5
Leadership Development and Organizational Maturity *Patricia Iannuzzi*	19
The Greening of Librarianship: Toward a Human Resource Development Ecology *Duncan Smith*	37
Perceptions of Library Leadership in a Time of Change *Peter V. Deekle* *Ann de Klerk*	55
Library Assistants in the Year 2000 *A. Ann Dyckman*	77
Recognition of the Role of the Librarian: Position Classification at Yale *Jack A. Siggins*	91
The Rhetoric of Performance Management: A Training Problem and Two Solutions *George Soete*	107

Introduction

The 1990's is a decade of decision for librarianship. The changes brought about by extensive use of technology, the continuous explosion of information, reductions in funding to support library services and programs, and rising costs of library materials are some of the forces that have and will continue to affect the work performed in libraries. One of the greatest challenges that academic and research libraries face today is to prepare the staff who work in those organizations for the future.

Preparation of staff requires serious attention to the human resource programs in our libraries and consideration of the needs and interests of all levels of staff, from the director to the entry level library assistant. Human resources planning requires a strategic approach, one which both focuses on the immediate issues and considers future needs. Library managers and administrators need to be adept at identifying the human resources issues in their organizations; able to design and implement programs, policies and procedures to address these issues in a timely and meaningful way; and willing to commit the necessary resources to support the full development of all staff.

An effective human resources strategy for the next century requires a firm understanding of the external forces and internal developments that affect staff in libraries, a framework for addressing human resources issues as important organizational concerns, and a set of specific actions to be taken to achieve desired results. The writings that follow offer a variety of perspectives on human resources management and what is needed to prepare staff at all levels for their future role and contribution in academic libraries.

In the first article, Susan Jurow, Director of the Office of Management Services of the Association of Research Libraries, discuss-

© 1992 by The Haworth Press, Inc. All rights reserved.

es the human resource management and development issues that must be addressed. She proposes several initiatives at both the organizational and staff level.

Patricia Iannuzzi offers a model of leadership development based on the library's organizational culture and level of development or maturity. She encourages the development of leadership throughout the library and suggests some strategies for doing so. In the next article, Duncan Smith addresses the need to rethink our approach to education for the profession, especially in the area of continuing education. He urges a "Green Movement" for librarianship and presents an action agenda for the creation of librarianship as a learning and self-renewing profession.

Two academic library directors, Peter V. Deekle and Ann de Klerk, report on the survey they administered to chief academic officers and library administrators at private liberal arts and comprehensive institutions about the role of the academic library director. Their findings suggest some areas of development for future library directors. Ann Dyckman, drawing on her experience as the Personnel Director of the Cornell University Library, discusses the changing role of library assistants and describes the steps libraries need to take to attract, retain, and develop support staff.

The two concluding articles describe practical experiences with the implementation of innovative human resource programs at two universities. Jack Siggins explains the process used to develop a new system for the classification of professional positions at Yale University. He offers his perspective on why librarians fared so well. George Soete tells about the training program used at the University of California, San Diego, Library to help librarians and other professionals learn how to do goals-based performance planning.

The authors of these articles suggest a set of general issues in human resource management and development and a variety of ideas and practices for developing staff at all levels in academic libraries to prepare for the 21st century. The discussion of these issues and the generation of many different and creative ideas needs to continue. As administrators, managers, librarians, and staff wrestle with their particular sets of problems and concerns, a broad understanding of a variety of models, approaches, and specific actions will be helpful.

Maureen Sullivan

Preparing Academic and Research Library Staff for the 1990's and Beyond

Susan Jurow

One definition of human resource management is "that area of organization life that focuses on the effective management and utilization of people."[1] This function is often understood to mean administrative activities such as recruitment, wage and payroll management, and benefits. Over the past forty years, however, a shift in the concept of management from control to development has led to a more inclusive definition of the human resources field. With a growing recognition of the key role staff play in the success of an organization,[2] it now encompasses those activities that promote greater job satisfaction and that support the development of individuals within the context of the workplace.

Some of the human resource management issues that face academic and research libraries are specific to librarianship and reside on a macro or profession-wide level. Recruitment of talented, qualified individuals to the profession, adequate pay for the level of knowledge and skill required by library work, and the nature of library education are three examples. For the most part, libraries and library staff compensate for the results of these broader problems by developing local initiatives. Until all the stakeholders agree to some form of collective action, library administrators and their staff will have to continue to mitigate their effects through individual efforts.

Susan Jurow is Director of the Association of Research Libraries Office of Management Services, Washington, DC.

© 1992 by The Haworth Press, Inc. All rights reserved.

Academic and research libraries generally have good programs and structures to manage the administrative aspects of a human resource program either because it is good management practice or because they are part of a larger institution that is required by law to do so. Libraries tend to have weaker programs and structures in human resources development areas, such as training and staff development and formal programs that lead to organizational renewal. Part of the problem is that human resource management and development has not been recognized as a priority in academic and research libraries, and it has been underfunded in the past. The practice has been to spend the lion's share of resources on fulfilling patron needs through the acquisition of more and better collections and services.

Investment in the improvement of the library's ability as an organization or its staff's ability as individuals to fulfill those needs is not a strategy that has been widely pursued. As a result, organizational and profession-wide infrastructures are not in place to meet current needs for human resource management and development, much less those that are anticipated.

HUMAN RESOURCE MANAGEMENT AND DEVELOPMENT PROGRAMS

Shelley Phipps, Associate Director for Science Libraries at the University of Arizona, reminds "that we are serving people in the educational process, we are linking people in the knowledge development process, and we are ultimately dependent on people to achieve progress in our efforts to improve and enhance access, storage, and preservation of the knowledge base."[3] Academic and research libraries and their staff face many challenges, including ongoing funding difficulties and anticipated changes in technology, demographics, and the flow of scholarly communication. Well-conceived programs and well-designed structures will be needed to improve and upgrade organizational capabilities and staff skills as these changes occur.

Some of the initiatives will be organizationally based and others will relate to improving personal or role effectiveness. The key human resource development issues will need to be addressed either through the creation of new programs or by making improvements to existing ones.

ORGANIZATIONAL INITIATIVES

From an organizational point of view, academic and research libraries have, for the most part, created effective structures for managing the administrative aspects of this function. Most of the libraries that are members of the Association of Research Libraries (ARL) have an individual, often either a librarian or personnel professional, designated to manage and act as liaison with the university or host institution for activities such as recruitment, payroll, and benefits.

Key organizational issues for the 1990s will revolve around the development of comprehensive human resource programs, the design and implementation of flexible, responsive organizational structures, and the nurturing of organizational cultures to sustain them.

Planning for Human Resource Management and Development

One key area of weakness in the human resource management process in academic and research libraries has been planning. Planning is a relatively new phenomenon for these libraries in general. Over the years, a number of studies have shown that, for a variety of reasons, academic and research libraries have not engaged in planning processes that would permit them to set goals, measure performance, and develop strategies for improvement.[4] This appears to be changing as more libraries engage in strategic planning.[5]

Business and industry have applied planning processes to human resource management both as a way of anticipating and responding to external forces and as a means of understanding and dealing with existing and emerging internal needs. To stay competitive, these organizations pay close attention to matching staffing levels with production and/or service goals and opportunities. This is obviously much more problematic for libraries that cannot generate more revenue even when an emerging need requiring more staff is identified.

In an era of shrinking resources, when libraries anticipate having to make choices among the many services and programs they would like to offer, rational human resource planning can be a valuable tool in the decision-making process. Carefully collected data and clearly conceived rationale will go a long way to helping garner stakeholder support when programs have to be terminated.

Performance planning, career planning, and training and development planning can be used to improve the effectiveness of existing staff. Establishing mutually developed goals and objectives can serve as a powerful communication device between the organization and the staff and between the manager and employee. They clarify direction and expectations, and they provide a mechanism for improvement. If a gap between goal and performance is seen as an opportunity for improvement rather than for punishment, planning, as embodied in the goal and objective setting process, provides a powerful organizational and individual learning device.

To make the most of the money available for training and staff development, careful planning is also required. William Tracey, a leading expert in the area of training systems design, recommends a systems approach.[6] This process begins with an analysis of needs and the collection of job data. Objectives and evaluative measures clarify the goals of the program. Materials, programs and participants are chosen based on the degree to which they fulfill the overall mission and goals of the organization. A systematic approach facilitates the level of accountability that is increasingly an expectation for not-for-profit organizations.

Organizational Structures

There are a number of ways to design a structure for an organization. The most common are either to use the industry standard, i.e., what everyone else uses, or to use a standard form, such as a pyramid hierarchy or teams. The shape of academic and research libraries as organizations is generally taken for granted. A new academic or research library is so seldom created that there is little experience with an organizational design process that matches the work that needs to be done with the most effective structure. Because every program or service already has its own constituency, there has also been a reluctance and resistance to questioning the need to continue an existing set of activities. As a result, reorganizations generally focus on moving an operation from one group to another.

With economic constraints as a feature for the foreseeable future, the pressure increases to question what an academic or research library does, how it does it, and for whom. This provides an opportunity for these libraries to rethink how they will organize staff and other resources in support of user needs. As more libraries engage in this process, a beginning point should be involving the people who do the work. It both takes advantage of the intelligence, energy, and expertise of staff and strengthens their commitment to the workplace.

The most important part of this rethinking process, however, will be the creation of structures that are capable of being self-renewing. With the rate of change that is anticipated, aligning tasks, goals, technology, communication needs, problem-solving needs, and decision-making requirements will require ongoing attention. Programs and services will have to be reviewed continually for relevance, and the organizational resources assigned to them reallocated as needs change. With staff as a resource, individuals will also have to be prepared to be redeployed. This will require a major shift in the way the staff think about their relationships to their jobs and to the organization for which they work. It will also require an increased commitment to retraining.

ORGANIZATIONAL CULTURE

The "culture" of an organization can be defined as "a pattern of basic assumptions–invented, discovered, or developed by a given group as it learns to cope with its problems of external adaptation and internal integration . . . taught to new members as the correct way to perceive, think, and feel in relation to those problems."[7] Culture is the basic system of values and beliefs that underlie and guide the choices and decisions that individuals in an organization make. Because it has generally not been discussed, it goes unrecognized as a force. It is often unclear why we do certain things other than because "that's how we do things here" or "we've always done it that way here."

Cultures can be built and supported in many different ways. One of the first opportunities libraries have to influence the thinking of staff is the orientation program. This program should go beyond a recitation of benefits and an overview of the departments of the library. If the library does not use this opportunity to begin instilling a sense of overall mission and purpose, then the employee is more vulnerable to the point of view of a counterproductive subculture.

Symbolic actions are a strong force in shaping culture. These may take the form of rituals that underscore the values of the organization as well as forms of relaxation that support a sense of community. Some of the symbolic activities in which libraries engage are staff award ceremonies, the use of the staff newsletter to recognize the achievements of an individual or a department, and annual meetings with the director. Playfulness can provide a different kind of opportunity for building culture. Summer barbecues, Christmas parties, and regular events like an annual bowling contest or skating outing become the means for strengthening relationships that must operate well in the workplace.

The role of culture has become more of an issue as academic and research libraries reexamine their mission and how they will fulfill it. The values and beliefs that support a collection-based library may not be the same as those needed to support an access-based one. Libraries that recognize such a key change will need to "manage" their cultures. This will require a clear understanding of what the culture supports and what it defends against. After comparing the current culture with what is needed to support the movement toward a desired future, attention will need to be paid to fostering a set of desired values and beliefs.

STAFF SKILLS INITIATIVES

It is important that programs focusing on an individual's ability to operate effectively in the work environment be seen as a partnership, a joint responsibility of the library and the individual involved. Human resource initiatives that focus on the individual need to be divided into two categories: those that focus on supervisors and managers, and those that relate to staff as individual members of their organizational community.

The Challenges to Managers

In their recent book on the workforce in the year 2000, Loden and Rosener suggest that "developing cooperative and committed work groups in which diversity is respected and supported will be a major task for corporate society during the next decade."[8] This will be no less true for academic and not-for-profit organizations. The three key words or phrases in this statement are developing, work group and diversity. They pinpoint the strategic issues for librarians and library staff with management and supervisory responsibility in the 1990s.

Even in the most enlightened of management models, managers and supervisors have relied on control as a means of "accomplishing work through others," the traditional definition of management. Control might have taken the form of autocratic or prescriptive behavior as it was practiced in early bureaucratic organizations, or it might be participatory as it is seen today in organizations that recognize the benefits of jointly-developed goals and objectives. In the end, however, control models rely on policies, rules, rewards, punishments, and oversight of work to ensure a satisfactory level of performance.

In a period of shrinking resources, "satisfactory" performance is no longer enough. Every library needs the wholehearted effort of each employee to get everything done that needs to get done. The question library managers are facing is how to obtain that level of performance. Some of the most effective strategies appear to be those that focus on developing employee commitment to results by increasing a personal sense of ownership.[9] Some of the strategies being used are: involving staff in organizational planning, problem-solving and decision-making through teams and groups, profit-sharing and pay for performance strategies, and self-managed work groups.

Some of these strategies are relatively unavailable to academic and research libraries, such as profit-sharing and pay-for-performance. A few libraries have begun to experiment with organizational strategies, including the development of collateral structures that permit staff to participate in organizational planning and decision-making, and with self-managed teams.[10]

Coaching is one of the most powerful tools for the individual manager or supervisor in improving performance. It is through this process that the employee can learn how to learn and develops the kind of commitment to personal development that leads to continuous improvement. Through regular, one-on-one conversations with a staff member, a manager can help the individual develop problem-solving skills, increase their sensitivity to organizational issues and constraints, improve technical competence, and identify the means for improved performance.[11]

Libraries are using many kinds of groups in the workplace, both to improve personal satisfaction and to improve organizational problem-solving. Library staff are often expected to participate in both short-term task forces with a specific task to accomplish and their primary work groups to which they contribute on an ongoing basis. The need for library managers and supervisors, as well as individual library staff, to be adept at working with groups will become more critical in the future. With the increased expectation of participation in the workplace and the increased complexity of problems requiring diverse points of view for solution, groups will become evermore a fact of organizational life.

Because an enormous amount of time and effort is spent in working with groups in libraries, it is critical that adequate preparation be provided to those who are expected to manage these groups. Arthur Van Gundy, a researcher in the area of group problem-solving, suggests three primary areas that require training for optimal group performance.[12]

First, a group leader must know how to assess and use resources possessed by a group. Participants in a group may be chosen for a variety of reasons, and it is important to be aware of the nature of the contribution each can make to the process. Secondly, a group leader is responsible for establishing a climate where the creative potential of the group can emerge. Third, they must know how to structure the process, so that each member can play a productive role in the process. Training programs need to be established in libraries that make available training to staff who are expected to play this kind of leadership position in groups whether as a one-time or ongoing assignment.

In their book, *Managing the Workforce 2000*, David Jamieson and Julie O'Mara suggest that as diversity in the workforce grows, another key to improving performance will be individualizing the performance management in a way that "will awaken people to their individual strengths and unique perspectives."[13] As managers who have begun to work actively at developing skills that empower others already know, this will pose an ongoing challenge. This approach requires sensitivity and balance among the needs of the individual, the group, and the library as a whole. It is an approach that encourages change, and the manager who facilitates this process needs both training and organizational support to operate effectively in an environment with these expectations.

Developing the Individual

There are three areas that will require close attention by libraries creating human resource development programs tailored for the individual staff member: technology skills, interpersonal skills, and leadership.

"The human element is the critical facilitator or bottleneck to effective use of IT"[14] (information technology). To integrate effectively new technologies into the library, much more needs to be invested in technology training and education. Technology training means teaching people to use both the equipment and the software when they are needed to support or improve personal or organizational effectiveness. The time and energy of staff are too expensive to permit individuals to learn and make mistakes on their own. Systematic programs that ensure consistent use of compatible programs will be required to manage the fast pace of technological obsolescence and change.

Technology education is a broader concept that implies understanding of the conceptual framework in which technology exists, so that the individual can make intelligent decisions about when and how to employ it. While most system-wide decisions are made at the management level, staff have a valuable role to play in identifying needs and areas that could be improved through automation and other applications of technology. As with any other change in the workplace, staff participation in these kinds of decisions will make changes that much easier to accomplish.

Increasing interdependence and diversity in the workplace will require a greater level of skill in interpersonal relations in the future. Individual staff members will need to be capable of accepting and confronting differences without the constant mediation of a manager or supervisor. As members of groups, library staff will need to learn how to use their individual strengths to contribute most effectively to a decision-making or problem-solving session. The more interdependent work becomes, the more staff will have to rely on collaborative skills as a means of working with and influencing others.

These are skills, not necessarily naturally occurring traits. If library management expects staff to exhibit them in the workplace, then it has a responsibility to hire staff with these skills, to support those who have them, and to help those who may not have them to build competency in using them.

The concept of leadership is also changing, so that it is no longer the sole purview of managers and administrators. As society begins to move beyond the concept of "heroic leadership," [15] individual staff members will need to consider their personal responsibility for meaningful, creative change in the workplace. If libraries are to be successful into the next century, the work of thinking and acting positively about the future and setting constructive goals will need to be the responsibility of all members of the workplace community. Efforts must be made to encourage and support staff to play a significant role in articulating and establishing an optimistic agenda for the future of libraries.

FLEXIBILITY AND LEARNING

The greatest challenge that faces academic and research libraries, librarians, and staff is the ability to function effectively in a changing environment. Most people understand this to mean *controlling* change. There are indeed strategies that an organization or an individual can use to outline a change process to ensure a smooth transition from one form of operation to another. Much of the change that occurs today, however, and most of the change that is likely to occur in the future, is imposed. It is change that originates elsewhere; it is change over which an individual or even an institution can exert little control.

The last twenty years have given us a taste of life in a world of rapid, continuous change. The one thing upon which futurists and experts in every field can agree is that this turbulent discontinuity in our environment will continue well into the next century. It means that, rather than preparing for something in particular, organizations and individuals must simply, like a boy or girl scout, "Be prepared."

For libraries and library staff, being "prepared" will mean being flexible and capable of shifting quickly in response to changing conditions. They will have to learn how to make decisions and choices in the present about an unknown future. To accomplish this, a willingness to take risks and a positive personal and organizational attitude toward learning will have to be integrated into the value systems and into the cultures of these libraries. On an organizational and individual level, learning how to learn from both successful and unsuccessful initiatives will be a critical factor in the survival and success of this profession and its institutions.

CONCLUSION

ARL represents the 119 largest academic and research libraries in the United States and Canada. On average, salary and wages represent 50% of their operating budgets.[16] As an aggregate, this equals approximately $460,000,000. Given anticipated ongoing funding difficulties, it is critical that libraries get the best possible value from this major investment.

Library schools prepare professionals by providing them with a theoretical framework and the basic knowledge and skills to support the mission and tasks of the library as it currently exists and as it has existed in the past. Library staff come into libraries with a wide variety of backgrounds, experiences, and skills. In order to ensure continuing success, these knowledge and skill bases will have to be constantly updated as the nature of the work and the library as an institution change. This will require both financial resources for continuing education and development, and a sense of personal responsibility for learning and renewal.

A much larger investment in staff training and development and in organizational development will be necessary to create and support the value systems and cultures required to meet the challenges of the twenty-first century. If academic and research libraries wish to attract and retain staff capable of performing effectively in this new environment, much more will have to be done to support initiatives in this area.

NOTES

1. Walters, R.W. "HRM in Perspective," in Tracey, W.R., ed. *Human Resources Management and Development Handbook*. New York: AMACOM, 1983. p.7.

2. Fitz-Enz, Jac. *Human Value Management*. San Francisco: Jossey-Bass, 1990. Chapter 11.

3. Phipps, Shelley. "The Vision and the Voices: Creating the Learning Environment," in *ARL; a Bimonthly Newsletter of Research Library Issues and Actions*, no.154, January 4, 1991. p.3.

4. Booz, Allen and Hamilton. *Problems in University Library Administration*. Washington, D.C.: Association of Research Libraries, 1970. p.39, and Hyatt, J.A. and A.A. Santiago. *University Libraries in Transition*. Washington, D.C.: NACUBO, 1987. pp.6 & 15.

5. Gardner, J.G. *Strategic Plans in ARL Libraries*. SPEC Flyer #158. Washington, D.C.: Association of Research Libraries Office of Management Services, 1989.

6. Tracey, W.R. *Designing Training and Development Systems*. rev.ed. New York: AMACOM, 1984.

7. Schein, E.H. *Organizational Culture and Leadership*. San Francisco: Jossey-Bass, 1985. p.9.

8. Loden, M. and J.B. Reasoner. *Workforce America! Managing Employee Diversity as a Vital Resource*. Homewood, IL: Business One Irwin, 1991. p.8.

9. Kinlaw, D.C. *Coaching for Commitment: Managerial Strategies for Obtaining Superior Performance*. San Diego: University Associates, 1989. p.2.

10. Lowell, G.R. and M. Sullivan. "Self-Management in Technical Services: the Yale Experience," *Library Administration & Management*, v.4, no.1, Winter 1989.

11. Ibid, Kinlaw, pp.22-23.
12. Van Gundy, A. *Managing Group Creativity*. New York: AMACOM, 1984. pp.7-8. Another excellent book on working with groups is *Groups That Work (Those That Don't)*. J.R. Hackman, ed. San Francisco: Jossey-Bass, 1990.
13. Jamieson, D. and J. O'Mara. *Managing the Workforce 2000*. San Francisco: Jossey-Bass, 1991. p.83.
14. Keen, P.G. *Shaping the Future*. Cambridge, MA: Harvard Business School Press, 1991. p.117.
15. Manz, C. and H. Sims, Jr. "SuperLeadership: Beyond the Myth of Heroic Leadership," *Organizational Dynamics*, Spring 1991, p.18-35.
16. *ARL Statistics, 1989-90*. Washington, D.C.: Association of Research Libraries, 1991. p.32.

Leadership Development and Organizational Maturity

Patricia Iannuzzi

How do library administrators recognize, encourage and nurture leadership potential throughout the organization?

Drawing upon current leadership research and theories of organizational maturity, and expanding upon themes in management and library literature, the author urges the development and implementation of strategies to develop leadership potential. Furthermore, the author recognizes and explores the role library administrators hold for creating the proper environment to nurture leadership potential. Successful leadership development is contingent upon organizational maturity. Certain mechanisms will only be successful at specific points during the organization's development.

The library profession devotes much discussion and research on the need to develop leaders. Libraries are bombarded by a wide range of external pressures not unlike those making a drastic impact in the for-profit arena: rapid growth, intense competition, unstable economic base, technological innovation at an exponential rate with costs escalating at almost an equal rate. The world is a more complex place, and librarianship has a critical need for imaginative and skilled leaders to navigate the course in a rapidly changing and complex society.

Leadership at the senior level, however, is not enough. As the business community now recognizes the need to unleash staff potential throughout the organization and to tap the wellspring of talent that we call human resources, so must libraries explore

---

Patricia Iannuzzi is Head of Reference at Florida International University, Miami, FL.

© 1992 by The Haworth Press, Inc. All rights reserved.

mechanisms to nurture leadership potential at all levels in the organization. Libraries must continue to experiment, to try new organizational models and encourage risk taking at all levels.

The mechanisms designed to encourage leadership potential must be applied within the proper framework and time line. In human development maturation points parallel the ability to learn certain concepts. Within libraries, organizational maturity parallels the ability to develop and support a particular leadership strategy. A particular strategy may be inappropriate for a library that has developed or "outgrown" the need for that particular approach. Application of a strategic approach at the incorrect time may produce more harm than good, potentially raising staff expectations while leaving staff frustrated and disenchanted.

This article will:

- Summarize strategies applied by leaders in our profession designed to create an environment conducive to nurturing leadership.
- Propose a theory for organizational maturity based on tenets in the corporate model but applicable to libraries.
- Demonstrate how organizational culture, vision and values can be measures of a library's organizational maturity.
- Caution library leaders to draw upon their powers of perception and proceed with sensitivity as they experiment with formal and informal mechanisms to create an environment where leadership is a shared responsibility.

The purpose of this discussion is to provoke debate and inspire further investigation. Librarians should derive additional insight as to why well-intentioned, innovative strategies sometimes fail in organizations. Finally, this essay should induce all library administrators to manage and reduce risk as they cultivate a solid understanding of the health and well being of their organizations.

NURTURING LEADERSHIP POTENTIAL

Libraries are not sheltered from the turbulence and instability of the world economy. Libraries of all types have a critical need for leaders who can succeed within a global arena. Library leaders must be "politicians" who can fulfill their role as advocates by forging appropriate partnerships and coalitions in support of their services; "innovators" who can participate in the design of information systems as the technology evolves; "managers" who can maintain a secure infrastructure for operations; and most of all, "visionaries" who possess the vision for libraries in the next millennium, and who have the skills to inspire others to commit to that vision.

Many library leaders are well aware that people are the greatest resource available, and libraries have begun to experiment with a variety of mechanisms to cultivate leadership potential throughout the organization. Some libraries have heeded Sheila Creth's suggestions to articulate an " . . . organizational expectation [that] moves toward assuring that the full capacity of staff talent and energy is reaped in addressing future challenges."[1] Creth presents the concept of shared leadership whereby staff will participate in the determination of " . . . *what* the library will become as well as participating in the implementation and management of that future."[2] In this article, the phrase leadership development refers to developing this potential in staff as opposed to the development of leaders for senior library positions.

Susan Jurow draws upon research conducted by the Center for Creative Leadership, in Greensboro, North Carolina, to develop a list of activities that will enhance the development of leadership competencies among staff. Jurow lists desired leadership traits and offers suggestions for activities to help individuals realize their potential or develop a particular skill. The emphasis is on developmental activities as opposed to skills attainment. The competencies that she identifies include:

- Visionary potential
- Ability to enlist others
- Confidence and encouraging trust
- Risk taking potential
- Empowering skills

For each competency, Jurow offers several developmental experiences that can help the creative and motivated administrator provide the situation to foster learning.[3] The suggestion is made here that certain situations foster the development of leadership competencies, and that academic library directors often employ these structures through formal and informal systems.

MECHANISMS TO ENCOURAGE LEADERSHIP DEVELOPMENT

Creative and innovative library administrators employ a wide range of mechanisms designed to create an organizational climate that encourages leaders. Strategies are most obvious during a shift in administration, often coupled with the introduction of a new management style and perhaps a different set of values. Strategies are also evident, if more subtle, in organizations where the senior administrator enjoys a lengthier tenure.

In some cases, the strategy is a conscious effort to convey a management style or philosophy, or to create a culture where staff "buy in" to certain values. In such organizations, the library director is primarily concerned with managing the culture: articulating organizational values, demonstrating a management style that is emulated throughout the organization, and insuring that individual and departmental goals and objectives are in sync with the overall library's goals and objectives.

The following list includes some mechanisms already in place in many libraries. Details relate ways in which the staff member is presented with the learning environment conducive to the acquisition of the desired leadership competency.

Task Forces/Committees

The use of task forces or committees is a common method of underscoring the individual's responsibility for the well-being of the library. Task forces that cut across hierarchical and departmental boundaries send a strong message that individuals are expected to move beyond the parochial interests of their department to assume responsibility in a broader sense for the development of a product or service. Participating in the decision-making process through task force membership also fosters identification with the end product and increases the possibility of commitment and support for the decision.

Task forces provide excellent opportunities to reward individuals by giving them a chance to make a visible contribution and to develop specific skills as they work together with their colleagues. Chairing such a group provides an additional opportunity for the organization to nurture the potential of a specific staff member by providing a special learning experience.

Through task forces individuals with varying skills, interests and viewpoints come together and learn from others, ultimately producing a better product from the shared effort. Individuals learn to appreciate diversity, and to confront differences in positive ways, managing conflict as the team grows.

Coordinator Positions

Libraries have continued to increase the number of "coordinator" positions in recent years. Individuals may observe that the coordinator title bestows all the responsibility but none of the authority in meeting a specific objective. Such positions, however, provide an excellent opportunity for the individual to develop certain leadership skills.

Citing leadership studies, Jurow suggests that "'inspiration' is the most difficult competency to learn." Jurow states that the leadership trait to inspire "relates most closely to communication and influencing skills."[4]

Committee assignments and coordinator responsibilities are two formal methods of providing staff with the setting to influence their peers. Both structures eliminate the crutch of authority and force individuals to rely on or develop their communicating and influencing skills to enlist support and persuade others. Both types of experience provide the opportunity for developing confidence in oneself and to earn the trust of others, another of the desired leadership competencies.

Promotion/Reward Systems

The formal structure for promotion, evaluation and/or financial reward is one of the most powerful administrative tools for communicating organizational values and expectations to staff. The promotion/reward system defines the model for individual behavior and serves as a mechanism to reward those who succeed within that model. The process of evaluating an existing system or designing a new system provides the forum for discourse and debate that can lead to an articulation of shared values. The process also identifies those individuals who do not "buy in" or share organizational values. The identification of individuals who possess fundamental conflicts with the organization is a painful yet imperative step in the process required to help individuals change attitudes or find an organization whose values they share.

The development of a promotion/reward system is often one of the most personally difficult processes for a library staff. The process affects all librarians, in their egos as well as in their pocketbooks. The promotion model reflects values and philosophies of professionalism and it ultimately defines the structure that rewards achievement. Participation in the development of such a model would provide a very special learning experience. This situation also creates an environment to test leadership competencies.

Organizational Design and Reorganization

Another of the more powerful and certainly more dramatic tools at the prerogative of library administrators is the organization structure. Organizational design determines patterns of work flow and communication. The structure can either facilitate movement for individuals across lines, or obstruct such movement. Virtually all libraries have experimented with the traditional organizational structure.

Some libraries are experimenting with matrix models and flatter hierarchies. Several technical services areas have reorganized into quality circles or self-managing work groups. Public service areas began with an increase in coordinator titles and they are still grappling with the best way to handle the multiple reporting lines for selectors/bibliographers/curators/reference staff. Other libraries opt to superimpose a committee structure over the hierarchy, with varied degrees of authority.

This "opening up" of the organization underscores the individual's responsibility to the library as a whole and creates opportunities for potential leaders throughout the organization to build networks. Rosabeth Moss Kanter emphasizes the importance of mobility in support of "network formation,"[5] a key concept in innovative organizations. She states that:

> Corporate entrepreneurs often have to pull in what they need for their innovation from other departments or areas, from peers over whom they have no authority and who have the choice about whether or not to ante up their knowledge, support, or resources, to invest in and help the innovator.[6]

Kanter asserts that innovators often succeed because of their relationships with peers throughout the organization. Although true innovators/leaders will find ways to develop their networks, an organization can facilitate these efforts by providing more opportunities to bring staff together across departmental and hierarchical lines. Such organizations create the environment for potential leaders to develop such competencies as the ability to enlist others, empowering skills, and perhaps risk-taking potential.

Projects/Acting Positions/Job Rotations/Internships

Another indication of an open organization is the opportunity for alternative staff assignments. The literature abounds with a wide array of programs established by libraries to encourage staff development within organizations. Examples include decisions to: assign staff to work on large projects; move staff between departments in order to assume temporary or acting positions; encourage job rotations between areas of the library; and the creation of internship opportunities. These experiences have a common element: the individual is removed from his/her regular assignment and put in a new position for a certain period of time. Each experience presents the challenge of learning new operational areas of the library. All foster mutual respect and understanding between library departments and create the need for the individuals involved to emphasize and to develop interpersonal skills.

These mechanisms provide the opportunity to develop several leadership competencies. The mechanisms contribute to the development of visionary potential by providing a broader knowledge base of library procedures, operations, and challenges. Internships, especially, and the resulting mentoring relationship, encourage the cultivation of vision. Acting positions can provide a supervisory experience for an individual whose current position does not provide this opportunity. This situation would support the development of "empowering skills" and "the ability to enlist others." Assuming complete responsibility for a project, whether it entails the development of a new service or the analysis and restructuring of an existing one, often requires the use of planning, budgeting, and analytical skills. More importantly, however, the change empowers the individual with complete responsibility for success or failure. Either situation contributes to the development of "the ability to take risks."

Formal Staff Development Programs

Academic libraries have long emphasized the need for ongoing training and skills development. Today, the ever-increasing rate of change and the resulting dynamics inherent in rapid change emphasize the need for varied staff development programs. Library staff can now benefit from programs designed to help the individual function successfully in an environment where the only constant is change. In addition to technical skills, librarians learn team building, active listening, conflict management, and problem solving skills.

Staff development programs are an excellent vehicle for communicating a management style or philosophy. Increasingly, academic libraries are developing in-house staff development programs, are bringing in library consultants who offer workshops or planning retreats, or sending staff to established development programs such as those offered by the Association of Research Libraries' Office of Management Services. An organization's commitment to an ongoing staff development strategy reflects its commitment to the individual as a unique and valuable resource.

Strategic Planning Process

The quantity, type, source, and pace of change require libraries to engage in strategic planning processes. In some cases, the strategic planning process is maintained within the administrative offices, and the emphasis lies with the production of tangible product, such as a planning report submitted to a Board of Trustees or a university administrator. In many instances, the strategic planning process includes participation of librarians throughout the organization and is used as a tool to articulate the library's vision and to encourage staff to share that vision. The process is a blueprint for the organization's goals and objectives and determines the framework for both departmental and individual goal-setting. A system-wide strategic planning process is an excellent example of a formal mechanism that creates the learning climate for two of the leadership competencies: developing visionary potential and developing the ability to enlist others.

In order for a strategic plan to be effective in the long term, staff must be personally involved. Staff must develop a degree of ownership for the plan and be committed to the plan's success. This process, aside from producing a better product, creates the opportunity for staff to initiate and complete complementary strategic planning processes at other levels of the organization. This process creates yet another leadership learning situation in which the individual can develop visionary potential, empowering skills, and the ability to enlist others.

These strategies and others are available to library administrators who attempt to create an environment that nurtures leadership potential. Although such mechanisms create opportunities to develop one or more leadership competencies, success is not guaranteed and without proper timing and follow through, the final result may be a failure. In order to understand these failures, a review of the library's mechanisms, within the broader framework of the organization's level of maturity is recommended.

ORGANIZATIONAL MATURITY–
A NATURAL PROCESS OF EVOLUTION

Although there is considerable discussion of the concept of organizational evolution in the management literature, library literature offers far less debate on this important topic. Theories developed in the for-profit sector do provide a useful insight to the library setting.

One interesting model proposed by Larry E. Greiner and evaluated by Paul Hersey and Kenneth Blanchard offers five stages of organizational growth.[7] Each phase leads to a crisis point, the resolution of which leads to the next phase of growth. Greiner calls these periods of "evolution" and "revolution," where "each revolutionary period is characterized by the dominant management style used to achieve growth, while each revolutionary period is characterized by the dominant management problem that must be solved before growth will continue."[8]

Greiner's five stages relate to the size, complexity and age of the organization:

1. Growth through *creativity* with the crisis of leadership

    Creative entrepreneurial leaders cannot cope with management problems as organization grows in size and complexity.

2. Growth through *direction* with a crisis of autonomy

    New leadership takes responsibility for managing and setting direction, but eventually lower level managers want more autonomy.

3. Growth through *delegation* with a crisis of control

    Response to desire for autonomy is to decentralize authority and decision-making which heightens morale and motivates staff, but which leads to possibility of top managers feeling like they've lost control.

4. Growth through *coordination* with a crisis of red tape

    In order to put more control in the hands of top managers, there is a return to centralization which staff resent, so the solution tends to be formal coordination structures; but the organization grows too large to run through coordination and gets slowed down by red tape.

5. Growth through *collaboration* with a crisis not yet determined

To cut red tape, the collaboration phase emphasizes team management and development of skills to deal with interpersonal conflict; but Greiner anticipates that the crisis for this phase will "center around the 'psychological saturation' of employees who grow emotionally and physically exhausted by the intensity of teamwork and the heavy pressure for innovative solutions."[9]

Another theory for organizational evolution is a model proposed by Edgar H. Schein.[10] Schein draws upon the research of anthropologists, sociologists, and psychologists to define organizational culture and to create a model of how culture affects the functions of the organization as it develops. Similar to Greiner's five stages of growth, Schein proposes three phases, but he defines these phases in terms of organizational culture. For each of Schein's three phases (organizational infancy, mid-life, and maturity), Schein describes symptoms of the organization's culture, asserting that "certain mechanisms of change will have particular relevance at certain stages of development."[11]

Since certain mechanisms to manage change will only be effective at certain stages of development, and since the developmental stages are defined in terms of the organizational culture, it can be concluded that the organizational culture must be understood and managed in order to effect change.

Schein and Greiner's models both acknowledge the importance of organizational culture in the evolution of the organization. Although Greiner's model does not explicitly mention culture, it is based upon key components of the organization's culture: management style, communication patterns, attempts to organize and reorganize to achieve desired objectives, and the desire to create an environment that motivates staff. These are, among others, elements of an organization's culture. Schein's model for organizational evolution includes the notion that culture is a "necessary glue in the growth period."[12] Both Shein's and Greiner's models for organizational development point to the importance of organizational culture as a determinant of organizational growth.

CULTURE

Organizational culture is a very difficult concept to define yet understanding this concept is crucial to effective leadership. Schein suggests that the "only thing of real importance that leaders do is to create and manage culture."[13] Others in the management literature link leadership with corporate culture, assigning the task of creating a strong culture as one of the most important responsibilities of leadership. Bryman notes that "the true leader needs to be a visionary who is capable of establishing a culture. . . . "[14] Bryman further asserts that "the absence of a strong culture can lead to severe problems."[15] John Gardner believes that " . . . leaders must understand the culture. But much of the culture is latent. It exists in the minds of its members. . . . "[16]

The management literature draws upon the research of various disciplines in an attempt to capture the essence of an organization's culture: how it evolved and what it does. Most definitions only include elements that reflect the culture of the organization. Some say that culture is reflected by rituals (or organizational routines), behaviors (or norms), and values.

On the other hand, Schein defines culture as:

> a pattern of basic assumptions–invented, discovered, or developed by a given group as it learns to cope with its problems of external adaptation and internal integration–that has worked well enough to be considered valid and, therefore, to be taught to new members as the correct way to perceive, think, and feel in relation to those problems.[17]

Over time the culture becomes imbedded in the infrastructure of the organization and may even be taken for granted. It is all that is implied by the phrase "this is how we do it."

VISION, CULTURE, AND ORGANIZATIONAL MATURITY

Any theory of organizational maturity in the library environment must include elements that contribute to the creation and management of the library's culture. These elements include organizational values, management styles, norms, patterns of communication, and philosophy of service. The degree to which staff share in these elements will determine the level of the library's cultural maturity. Organizational maturity can be related to stages of vision: conceptualizing, communicating (inspiring), and creating the environment (culture) where staff share the vision and are committed to it.

Conceptualization and Articulation

The words "leader" and "vision" are often coupled. We want leaders to have vision. They should be able to draw upon a broad knowledge base of skills and experience to describe the future. The vision should reflect an effective analysis of the current situation and clearly articulate future direction.

Communication and Inspiration

Librarians who possess a vision are not necessarily leaders. There are many great thinkers with vision who lack the skills to articulate a vision in a way that inspires. Successful communication of a vision involves more than developing mission statements or a strategic plan. Communication is a much broader and more complex process. Leaders must communicate the organizational vision continually and in ways that motivate and inspire. This vision must become part of the infrastructure of management as well as part of the organizational culture.

Creating the Environment Where Each Individual Can Pursue That Vision

When an organization has a leader with vision; when that vision is woven into the fabric of organizational life; when staff share it and when programs reflect it; when the direction is set and all are on the same course; then, it is time to create the environment where all can pursue it. In this environment, the organizational culture is strong. A symbiotic relationship exists, in that the vision is reflected in the organizational culture and the organizational culture facilitates the realization of the vision. This is the "excellent company" where values are shared described by Peters and Waterman.[18]

The mature organization can be identified by certain characteristics such as: (1) the management style of the director is adopted throughout the organization; (2) programmatic objectives are in sync with organizational mission; (3) individual goals and objectives reflect departmental and organizational goals; (4) management style and philosophy are imbued in staff development programs; (5) a structure that decentralizes power through budget and decision-making mechanisms; and (6) the existence of an umbrella culture and/or subcultures.

An evaluation and understanding of each of these cultural attributes will provide broader understanding of the academic library's level of organizational growth. Some questions to ask are:

- Is the management style of the director and senior administration evident throughout the organization, or are there areas of different, perhaps conflicting, styles in practice?
- Is the organizational mission clearly stated with programmatic objectives in sync; or is there contradiction between the mission and the services that are in place?
- Do individual goals and personal expectations reflect departmental priorities which in turn reflect organizational priorities, or is the individual excluded from the goal-setting process?
- Is the organization's culture strong and unified in order to support decentralizing power and decision-making through the budget process; or is it too great a risk to allocate budget responsibility to departments because of parochialism and self-interest?
- Generally, is there a strong, uniform sense of how the organization works, with values that are shared by all and with a common understanding of direction and purpose; or are there pockets of dissent, disagreement and/or conflict with regard to values and philosophy of purpose?
- Has there been an emphasis on staff development? How extensively and how consistently? Do supervisors and department heads embrace their role as agents for staff develop-

ment; or is the responsibility for staff development removed from the supervisory role?

TIMING: SENSITIVE PERIODS IN AN ORGANIZATION'S DEVELOPMENT

It has been demonstrated that a group of mechanisms is available to encourage the development of leaders. These mechanisms include: committee structures, coordinator responsibilities, planning processes, staff development programs, and promotion and reward systems. Why, then, do these mechanisms sometimes fail?

In order for these strategies to be successful, library administrators must be attuned to the level of organizational readiness. The administration must have honest answers to the questions posed above.

Schein stresses this view of organizational readiness:

> The kind of change that is possible depends not only on the developmental stage of the organization but on the degree to which the organization is unfrozen and ready to change . . . certain mechanisms of change will have particular relevance at certain stages of development.[19]

Following are some situations that may fail if the organization is not ready:

- The Director and senior administration advocate an environment where change is viewed as opportunity, where innovation is encouraged, and where risk-taking and experimentation is supported. This philosophy is articulated from the top, through written products, presentations, and in recruitment literature. A major department head (middle manager) is a conservative manager who doesn't want to make waves. He or she discourages new ideas, is offended by junior staff questioning assumptions, and stifles any attempt to try something new or different. A reluctance to work with or confront middle managers may send a mixed message to the staff.

- The administration structures a complex planning process which includes participation from all staff. The task requires a large amount of organizational energy and commitment. The product will be an articulation of library priorities. In one organization this may be a successful mechanism to build consensus, work through differences, and create a shared vision for services. In another, it may create frustration because the vision is already shared, i.e., the staff already feel in sync with the library's overall priorities. Staff are frustrated by the lack of resources and they resent the amount of organizational time and energy "wasted" on talking about something that is perceived as unrealistic.
- A library administration recognizes the desirability of including staff in the decision-making process. In order to encourage communication and to take advantage of individual skills throughout the organization, a task force structure that cuts across hierarchical and departmental lines is established. Unfortunately, there has not been a strong tradition of committee assignment in this organization. Any of the following may occur: individuals do not understand their roles and responsibilities as members of a committee; chairs do not possess facilitating skills to bring together diverse opinions; some department heads may verbalize their opinion that such committees are a waste of time and are unsupportive; or the administration responds slowly or accepts only part or none of the recommendations without communicating the rationale for the decision back to the committee.

Library administrators should not be discouraged from continuing to explore ways to create a climate for leadership development. To the contrary, there are far too few library directors willing to take the risks that are necessary to experiment with various strategies. As Herbert S. White asserts:

> For libraries, oriented toward tradition and risk avoidance to a greater extent than most organizations and without the incentive of profits to justify chance taking, the temptation to hire a long line of inoffensive looking "grey" people is just

about insurmountable. Nowhere is this pattern clearer than in the hiring of administrators for major academic libraries.[20]

Although we have our share of 'grey people' in administrative positions in libraries, we also have a core of energetic and visionary leaders who want to nurture the spirit of creativity and innovation within their organizations. Library literature and library management training programs reflect an emphasis on leadership development. We need the leaders in senior positions who will continue to strive to create the culture where staff are encouraged to perform to their potential, where we embrace change and see the opportunities in the chaos that surrounds us. We need library leaders who not only have vision, but who are skilled and committed to creating the environment where that vision is shared.

REFERENCES

1. Sheila D. Creth, "Organizational Leadership: Challenges Within the Library," in *Leadership for Research Libraries,* ed. Anne Woodsworth and Barbara Von Wahlde (Metuchen, N.J.: Scarecrow Press, 1988), 88.

2. Ibid, 89.

3. Susan Jurow, "Preparing for Library Leadership," *Journal of Library Administration,* 12, No. 2 (1990): 66-71.

4. Ibid., 67.

5. Rosabeth Moss Kanter, *The Change Masters: Innovation for Productivity in the American Corporation* (N.Y.: Simon and Schuster, 1983), 162-163.

6. Ibid., 162.

7. Paul Hersey and Kenneth Blanchard, *Management of Organizational Behavior: Utilizing Human Resources* (Englewood Cliffs, N.J.: Prentice-Hall, 1988), 356-358, citing Larry E. Greiner, "Evolution and Revolution as Organizations Grow," *Harvard Business Review,* (Jul/Aug 1972): 37-46.

8. Ibid., 356.

9. Ibid., 44.

10. Edgar H. Schein, *Organizational Culture and Leadership* (San Francisco: Jossey-Bass, 1985), 270-296.

11. Ibid., 283.

12. Ibid., 283.

13. Ibid., 2.

14. Alan Bryman, "Leadership and Corporate Culture," Management Decision, 24, no. 6 (1986): 51.

15. Ibid.

16. John W. Gardner, "Leadership Development," *New Management*, (1988): 16.

17. Schein, 9.

18. Thomas J. Peters and Robert H. Waterman, Jr., *In Search of Excellence: Lessons from America's Best-Run Companies* (N.Y.: Warner Books, 1983), 76.

19. Schein, 271.

20. Herbert S. White, "Entrepreneurship and the Library Profession," *Journal of Library Administration*, 8, no. 1 (Spring 1987): 14.

The Greening of Librarianship: Toward a Human Resource Development Ecology

Duncan Smith

Peter M. Senge opens his book *The Fifth Discipline: The Art & Practice of The Learning Organization* with the following statement:

> From a very early age, we are taught to break apart problems, to fragment the world. This apparently makes complex tasks and subjects more manageable, but we pay a hidden, enormous price. We can no longer see the consequences of our actions; we lose our intrinsic sense of connection to a larger whole.[1]

The profession's literature is filled with articles and editorials about library education and its current lamentable state. These articles tend, however, to break the problem apart and do not examine the profession's educational system. This article examines the library profession's educational ecology and concludes with some recommendations for strengthening this system. This examination consists of four components: an examination of another profession's educational ecology, a summary of three different futures-oriented views of the library profession, a general discussion of the current educational system, and a proposed "Green Movement" for the profession whose purpose is to address the weaknesses that exist in the current educational ecology. This

---

Duncan Smith is Continuing Education Coordinator, School of Library and Information Sciences, North Carolina Central University, Durham, NC.

article focuses on the continuing education component of the profession's educational system.

WHAT MARK TWAIN HAS TO SAY ABOUT LIBRARY EDUCATION

A few years ago a colleague was accepted to the School of Law at Duke University. In the packet of information sent from the university was a letter from the School's Dean. In her letter, the dean suggested some readings that new law students might wish to consider as they prepared to enter law school. One of the titles contained in the dean's recommended readings was Mark Twain's *Life on the Mississippi*. This title not only appeared on her suggested reading list, but was strongly recommended. In fact, the dean indicated that if a student was only going to read a single work to prepare for a legal education that work should be Mark Twain's *Life on the Mississippi*. The dean went on to state that she knew of no title that did a better job of describing what a professional education entails.

Life on the Mississippi was published in 1874. It describes how Mark Twain became a river boat pilot. The book opens with a description of the Mississippi River's history, its importance, and its most visible characteristic: its tendency to change. For the middle of America during the mid-1800s, the Mississippi was everything. The livelihood of the entire region depended on the river and the fact that it was navigable. What was true for the region was even more so for an individual. If a landowner's property bordered the river, he was wealthy. If his land did not border the river, he was not. In Twain's vision, wealth and poverty were determined by the simple fact of whether or not one owned river front property. The Mississippi, however, was constantly changing its course and one's fortune rose or fell according to these changes. Twain gives vivid descriptions about the river's changes and the personal and communal boons and busts that resulted.

After his opening chapters, Twain writes about his becoming a river boat pilot. In order to become a pilot, an individual had to find an experienced pilot who was willing to take on an apprentice or "cub" pilot. In Twain's case, he finds a Mr. Bixby who after much cajoling agrees to accept Twain as a cub. The bulk of Twain's education is spent in the pilot house next to Mr. Bixby "learning the river." In one of his first lessons, Twain learns that he just can't memorize landmarks as a way of knowing where he is on the Mississippi. Instead, he must learn the "shape" of the river because as Bixby points out, the river and its landmarks not only change but look different at different times. The way a dead oak looks on a bend during the day and the way the same dead oak looks on the same bend on a moonlit night are entirely different and, therefore, deceiving and likewise potentially disastrous. In essence, Twain discovers that, instead of learning the river's specifics, he must learn its dynamics. It is shortly after this particular lesson about the shape of the river that Twain says of his education:

> Two things seemed pretty apparent to me. One was, that in order to be a pilot a man had to learn more than any one man ought to be allowed to know; and the other was, that he must learn it all over again in a different way every twenty-four hours.[2]

Twain continues his discussion of his education by describing the community of learning that typified the river pilot profession. Because of the nature of the river, a pilot was constantly learning and relearning the river. This fact is discussed early on in the book when we learn that pilots who are not currently engaged or whose boats are lying in port usually accompany boats going down river to get a "fresh look" at the river before they begin taking their own boats down river. This was standard practice and a riverboat's pilot house was frequently filled with pilots. During these trips down river the pilots spent most of their time exchanging ideas and information about the river as well as commenting on each other's performance. This community of learning also manifested itself in one final way. The pilots formed an association. One of the main services of this association was the continuing education of its members.

All along the river wharf boxes were posted. All association members had keys to these boxes. Inside the boxes were reports of the conditions of the river. Of this service Twain says:

> The pilot who deposited a report in the Cairo box (after adding to it the details of every crossing all the way down from St. Louis) took out and read half a dozen fresh reports (from upward bound steamers) concerning the river between Cairo and Memphis, posted himself thoroughly, returned them to the box, and went back aboard his boat again so armed against accident that he could not possibly get his boat into trouble without bringing the most ingenious carelessness to his aid. Imagine the benefits of so admirable a system in a piece of river twelve or thirteen hundred miles long, whose channel was shifting every day! The pilot who had formerly been obliged to put up with seeing a shoal place once or possibly twice a month, had a hundred sharp eyes to watch it for him now, and bushels of intelligent brains to tell him how to run it. His information about it was seldom twenty-four hours old. If the reports in the last box chanced to leave any misgivings on his mind concerning a treacherous crossing, he had his remedy; he blew his steam-whistle in a peculiar way as soon as he saw a boat approaching; the signal was answered in a peculiar way if that boat's pilots were association men; and then the two steamers ranged alongside and all uncertainties were swept away by fresh information furnished to the inquirer by word of mouth and in minute detail.[3]

One of the things Twain does in *Life on the Mississippi* is give us a glimpse of the educational ecology of the river pilot profession. It is a system focused on preparing individuals to practice this profession. It is a system in which most of the learning is done at the point of practice. It is a system which acknowledges the need for the constant updating of its members' skills and knowledge. It is a profession that provides this updating at the point of practice and in a timely manner. It is also a profession that has established itself as a learning community where future river pilots are educated by experienced pilots at the point of practice and members of the profession assume the dual responsibilities of self-education and the education of their peers. This system is how one profession ensured that it had an ample number of members who were competent and qualified to steer an entire region's wealth through changing, if not troubled, waters.

AS THE CENTURY TURNS: LIBRARIANSHIP IN THE 1990s AND BEYOND

In the 1990s the library profession finds itself in waters that are both changing and troubled. The continued closing of library schools, an increase in the number of schools under review, and concern about the type of individuals who are choosing to enter the profession are some of the many factors that are fueling an increase in the amount of time and literature devoted to examining the library profession and its role in our society. Three documents which discuss this dilemma are: *Statement on the Decade of the Librarian 1990-2000, Information 2000: Library and Information Services for the 21st Century,* and *Strategic Vision for Professional Librarians.*

The *Statement of the Decade of the Librarian 1990-2000* was prepared as part of the American Library Association's strategic planning process. This document, which was approved by ALA Council at the 1991 annual meeting in Atlanta, opens with the following vision statement describing a librarian in the year 2000:

> The vision of the librarian in year 2000 is as a leader, a fighter, an expert, a partner, a model, and a professional. In order to achieve this vision we must reposition librarianship as the information profession in society by enhancing society's perception of librarians; each librarian must also take responsibility for his or her own self-image and professional definition: acting as professionals with a mission instead of employees with a job. Library employers must recognize their responsibility for investing in their personnel.[4]

This statement goes on to provide six strategic directions for ensuring that this profile of the librarian is realized. This vision is to be achieved by bringing the best people into the field, educating people for library/information careers, creating a work force that reflects a pluralistic society, compensating librarians at a more competitive level, keeping the librarians we have, and increasing recognition for librarians as information professionals in a changing society. The main focus of these strategies is the recruitment of "new blood" into the profession. In fact, it is only the fifth direction, "keeping the librarians we have," that is targeted at individuals who are currently practicing librarians.

The 1991 White House Conference on Library and Information Services identified three challenges for libraries in the near future.[5] These challenges were in the areas of literacy, productivity, and democracy. The summary report of this conference *Information 2000* contains a complete listing of the conference recommendations and library based solutions to the challenges facing our society in the three areas. The proposed solutions rely heavily on technology or related approaches to the provision of library and information services. The report is filled with requests for federal action, federal funding, partnerships, coalitions, the development of model programs, and the education and training of librarians. In fact, three of the ninety-five recommendations and petitions were directed specifically at personnel and staff development. These were: to study alternative delivery systems for providing access to master's level study; to provide scholarships, grants, and loans at all levels to support continuing education, staff development and training in library and information science; and to increase financial aid to attract minorities to the profession.[6] Here again, two out of three recommendations are geared to initial recruitment to the profession. It should also be pointed out that none of these recommendations was viewed as a high priority by the conference as a whole.

The document which contains the most sweeping recommendations for change in the profession is *Strategic Vision for Professional Librarians*, a statement developed by the Strategic Visions Steering Committee. This committee is composed of a group of library leaders who have been engaged in thoughtful discussion about the profession and its future. They are not affiliated with any organization. This group of concerned librarians, however, has developed a vision of the profession which makes a commitment to selecting and delivering information that users need at the point and moment of need; to educating users to manage information; to furthering the development of the "virtual library," a concept of information housed electronically and deliverable without regard to its location or to time; to taking responsibility for information policy development; and to experimenting with new forms of organizational structure and staffing within libraries to enable delivery of new types of services to users, especially remote users, or users of the growing "virtual library."[7] This document also has several recommendations about recruitment and development of the profession's work force. The following specific recommendations are made:

> Publicize the unique advantage at which the "information age" places librarians as information professionals.
>
> Strengthen the degree-granting programs, develop effective relationships with other information-related disciplines, and establish alternative models for attaining professional credentials.
>
> Attract and retain creative and innovative people.
>
> Incorporate different competencies/professionals into the emerging information delivery environment.
>
> Address the importance of continuing professional education.[8]

Again, four of the five recommendations deal with the recruitment of new blood or new talent to the field. It is only the last recommendation that addresses the need for the continuing education and development of existing personnel.

While each of these documents identifies different challenges for the profession and proposes somewhat different solutions to these challenges, they concur on two themes: they recognize that librarianship must change if it is to remain a viable and productive part of society; and they rely heavily on "new recruits" to the profession to carry out their proposed changes.

This strategy will not work. There are two compelling reasons why the "new recruit" strategy is doomed to failure. First, there are approximately 150,000 practicing librarians in this country.

This compares to the approximately 4,400 new librarians graduated each year by the ALA-accredited library schools in this country and Canada.[9] These 4,400 individuals, the "new blood" of the profession, will be hired, oriented, trained, supervised and acculturated to the profession by the 150,000 individuals who are currently members of it. Many of these 150,000 persons will reinforce the status-quo. By the time the "new blood" gets to any position of power or influence it will be virtually indistinguishable from the profession's status quo. Second, Kathleen Heim and William E. Moen surveyed students enrolled in accredited library and information science programs in the spring of 1988. They found that approximately 53% of all students had some library experience and that 34% had held a full-time position in a library.[10] They also found that for 88% of the 53% that had some library experience, this experience had had a positive influence on their decision to become librarians.[11] This means that at least half of the profession's new recruits are already partially acculturated to the profession prior to entering it. In fact, these individuals are choosing librarianship because they have some first-hand knowledge of it and like what they see. These two factors indicate that any new talent that enters the field is going to be exposed to an enormous amount of pressure to conform to existing practices, policies, and standards. Yet, the three documents described earlier all indicate that what is needed is a new vision of the profession that is complete with new practices, policies, and standards.

The repositioning of the library profession will not be achieved by recruiting new talent to the profession. The profession does not need new librarians as much as it needs *renewed* librarians. The repositioning of the library profession can only be achieved through the continuing education and development of existing staff.

CONTINUING LIBRARY EDUCATION: AN ECOLOGICAL PORTRAIT

The primary mode of continuing education in the library profession is the workshop. The workshop or conference has been indicated as the preferred mode of continuing education in a study of

Florida public library directors by McCrossan. This study asked public library directors in Florida to discuss which modes of professional development or continuing education had been most helpful to them. The results showed that 90% of respondents rated workshops as important or extremely important, while only 78% rated reading library science publications as important or extremely important, and 57% rated attending meetings of library associations as important or extremely important.[12] It is particularly interesting to note that in some ways the third most valued experience, attending professional association meetings, is very much like attending a workshop. This preference is not restricted to public library directors. In a study of its membership conducted in the spring of 1991, the Special Libraries Association concluded that two-thirds of its membership found the Association's professional development program a valuable service. This survey also asked members to indicate their interest in five types of educational services: seminars (workshops), self-study courses, videotapes, audiotapes, and in-house training/seminars.[13] The respondents provided the following rankings: 78% stated they would either definitely or probably attend an educational seminar, 52% expressed an interest in in-house training/seminars, and 43% expressed an interest in self-study. Though the self-study figure is high, it is still far behind workshops and in-house training, especially when you consider the fact that these two headings are similar. This preference for workshops is not new in the library profession. In her landmark study of continuing education, Betty Stone found that the three modes of continuing library education that received the highest use were attending professional meetings, participation in professional committees and attending workshops.[14] When one looks at how these same respondents rated the effectiveness of these modes, however, the profession's preference for workshops is again indicated with 74% of respondents identifying the workshop as an effective means of continuing education, while only 57% found professional meetings an effective means, and committee work was found to be an effective continuing education vehicle by only 43%.[15]

This preference for the workshop mode of continuing education is not limited to participants. Providers seem to prefer this mode as well. In a recent article in *Public Libraries*, a survey conducted by Blazek and Perrault indicated that 95% of responding state librarians viewed their institutions as having a responsibility for the continuing education of public library employees engaged in the provision of reference service. This same population indicated that the group workshop was the preferred means of addressing this need with the only exception being the evaluation of reference departments.[16] For this activity, state librarians preferred to use members of the library staff or contracted consultants. According to the *1992 Library and Information Science Education Statistical Report* the ALA-accredited library schools in the United States and Canada held over 153 workshops in 1990-91.[17] This is the most frequently used mode of continuing education provided by these schools. Other modes included colloquia/lectures (128), institutes/symposia/conferences (74), short courses (63), and seminars (58). All of these events are group activities that occur in an established, narrowly defined time period. They are in essence a sub-species of the genus workshop. In fact, the only two non-workshop formats on which data were collected are tutorials and other formats. In 1991, these formats only accounted for 10 activities.[18] The library profession's continuing education ecology, therefore, is dominated by a mode that is "event-focused."

One of the most attractive features of the workshop as a continuing education mode is that it enables one to leave if not the library at least the desk at which one works. This is itself a good thing since it allows the participant to focus on the workshop topic in an environment that is more conducive to learning and also limits the day to day distractions that impede learning in the workplace. While these factors may contribute to a conducive learning environment and while they may increase the learning that goes on in the workshop, they also decrease the likelihood that this learning will be successfully integrated as part of the participant's day to day work life. In their new book entitled *Transfer of Training*, Mary L. Broad and John W. Newstrom cite a study conducted by Timothy Baldwin and Kevin Ford. Baldwin and Ford analyzed the perceptions of human resource development professionals regarding the transfer of the content of management development programs. On the average, these professionals believed that only 40% of the content of programs they conducted was transferred to the work environment immediately after training, about 25% was still being applied six months later, and a mere 15% was still being used at the end of the year.[19]

In their article, "Improving Inservice Training: The Message of Research," Bruce Joyce and Beverly Showers provide a blue-print for workshops that work. These two authors examined over 200 studies on training effectiveness. Their conclusions are that in order for workshops to be effective they must incorporate a mixture of the following elements: presentation of theory and rationale, modeling or demonstration, practice under simulated conditions, structured feedback, and finally coaching in the use of the new skill or strategy.[20] To illustrate this point further, in a workshop where only theory and rationale are presented to participants, only 10 out of 100 participants will acquire the skills taught. In a workshop where participants receive both theory and rationale and have a number of opportunities to see the skill demonstrated, between 10 and 30 participants out of 100 will acquire the new skill. In a workshop where theory and rationale are presented and participants have a number of opportunities to see the skill demonstrated and get to practice the skills themselves with some feedback regarding their performance, between 80 and 90 participants out of 100 will acquire the skill.[21]

One of the best examples of the use of this information in librarianship is the State of Maryland's reference training program. In 1983, the Division of Library Development and Services of the Maryland State Department of Education hired a survey research firm to conduct a massive, unobtrusive study of reference performance in Maryland. Librarians in Maryland were able to answer reference questions accurately only 55% of the time, a result that is in keeping with other studies conducted in other locations. What was unique about the Maryland study, however, was that not only was reference accuracy measured, but the behaviors which contributed to it were also identified. Based on the results of this study, the Division of Library Development and Services developed a three-day training program that incorporated all of the approaches mentioned by Joyce and Showers. Librarians who received this training achieved 77% reference accuracy in a follow-up study while librarians who did not receive it only provided accurate answers 60% of the time.[22] More importantly, in two locations staff not only participated in the three-day training program but engaged in intensive peer coaching and intermittent coaching and received supervisory support. In the follow-up study, the librarians in these two locations provided accurate answers to reference questions an average of 95% of the time.[23] State-wide implementation of this training program resulted in a state-wide reference accuracy score of 65% in 1986 and 70% in 1990.

In addition to reassessing reference accuracy, the 1990 study also sought to determine which activities supported the continued use of behaviors that contribute to a complete and accurate answer. This aspect of the study was very important, since it was discovered that overall use of the model reference behaviors in the state had declined. This decline is consistent with what studies like those of Baldwin and Ford tell us about the effectiveness of workshop or event-oriented programs. Activities that supported the continued use of the model reference behaviors were a training program or event that provided sufficient time for participants to learn and practice the behaviors, peer coaching several times a week for at least one month after the training, and specific strategies for maintaining the model reference behaviors such as a reference policy requiring their use.[24] The study also pointed out that a combination of all three would have a significant impact on the continued use of these behaviors.[25]

The Maryland reference training program is an exemplary program. Yet, as the cited studies show, this training program alone does not result in continued application of new skills on the job. In this specific case, however, a great deal of thought, time, energy, and commitment have gone into ensuring that the model reference behaviors do indeed transfer to the workplace. The Maryland program was developed by a group of individuals who were extremely knowledgeable about adult learning and the development of continuing education activities. It is unfortunate that these skills are not more widespread in the profession.

During 1991, the Continuing Library Education Network/Round Table (CLENE/RT) and the Southeastern Library Network (SOLINET) conducted a survey of continuing education providers in the southeastern United States. A total of 134 continuing education providers and staff development officers responded to this survey. The following was revealed: 72% of respondents devoted less than 25% of their time to continuing education and staff development; 32% of these individuals have 3 years or less experience with continuing education; and 31% of these individuals have a wide-range of continuing education responsibilities.[26] This range is wide enough to indicate that these individuals have total program responsibility for continuing education and staff development in their organizations. For example, it was not unusual for an individual to indicate responsibility for managing, developing, coordinating, and supervising continuing education activities. In several cases, the respondents indicated that they also served as instructors in continuing education activities.

The individuals who responded to this survey were asked to participate in a focus-group sponsored by CLENE and SOLINET at the American Library Association's 1991 annual meeting in Atlanta. Approximately 30 individuals participated in this focus group, the purpose of which was to identify the continuing education needs of the region's continuing library educators. The top three needs identified by the participants were: assistance in identifying continuing education resources; continuing education program planning; and assistance in identifying needs assessment strategies and developing needs assessment competencies.[27]

Based on the evidence offered thus far, one can only conclude that librarianship has a continuing education ecology that is fragile and endangered. The library profession's continuing education ecology is event-focused. These events occur in organizations which do not have strong transfer of training programs in place. It is also a system that is managed by individuals with limited experience in continuing education and who do not give a significant portion of their time to it. All of this adds up to a system that, at best, can be minimally effective in producing significant and lasting change, such as that urged in the three documents discussed earlier in this article.

How then does librarianship achieve its goal of repositioning itself to be the information profession in society? If the "new blood" approach will not work and our continuing education ecology is toxic, how are we to achieve significant and lasting change in librarianship? The profession must-to borrow a phrase from the 60s-change the system.

A GREEN MOVEMENT FOR THE PROFESSION

In her article, "Staff Development: Where Do We Go From Here?" Sheila Creth states that if she were conducting a performance evaluation for the library profession in staff development she would be inclined to give it a "C-" with many libraries deserving a failing grade and only a very few deserving an "A."[28] This author certainly supports Creth's assessment. Several groups, however, are working to strengthen the profession's continuing education ecology. The Association of Research Libraries through its Office of Management Services conducts a Training Skills Institute.[29] This institute is designed to aid in the development of in-house training programs by developing the training competencies of its participants. The Library of Congress's Technical Processing and Automation Instruction Office has developed a 30-hour train-the-trainer program. This program was field-tested and evaluated at Simmons College during the spring of 1990.[30] The Library of Congress is currently revising this program and is considering offering it to the library community at large. Here again, this effort is aimed at strengthening the system by developing the talent that is latent within it. CLENE has also begun a long-range and strategic planning process whose purpose is to identify ways for CLENE to strengthen and support the profession's continuing education system.

Strengthening the existing system, however, will not be enough. In order to produce change of the magnitude contained in the *Statement on the Decade of the Librarian*, *Information 2000*, and *Strategic Visions for Professional Librarians*, the profession needs to reorient its efforts. What is needed is a continuing education system that resembles the one described by Twain. This is one in which learning occurs at the point of practice; that uses the talents of experienced practitioners to educate and train new or inexperienced staff; and that develops a culture in which individuals assume responsibility for their own growth and the growth of their colleagues. What is needed is a system that embodies some of the principles advocated by the Green Movement.

The Greens are best known for their pro-environment policies. These polices are ultimately aimed at providing a safe and reasonable environment in which human beings can work and achieve fulfilling lives. Taking direction from the Greens, this article concludes with a framework for achieving a safe and reasonable environment in which librarians can work and achieve fulfilling lives. The proposed "Green Movement in Librarianship" would be based on the following principles:

1. Human beings are self-renewing resources.
2. Human beings require a safe, nurturing environment in which to renew themselves.
3. Organizations, agencies, policies or individuals who do not actively create safe and nurturing environments actively work against self-renewal. There is no neutral ground.
4. Each individual is responsible for his or her own renewal.
5. Each individual is responsible for the renewal of his or her colleagues.

The following strategies would form an action agenda for a Green Movement in the profession:

1. Librarians should become informed consumers of continuing education. Librarians should learn to distinguish a good workshop from a bad one. Librarians should provide specific feedback to providers about what worked and what did not, what was helpful and what would be more helpful.
2. Efforts to develop competent and highly skilled continuing education practitioners in librarianship should be increased and expanded.
3. Transfer of training strategies should be in place in the profession. All elements of the system–participants, supervisors, employing organizations, trainers and sponsoring organizations–must assume responsibility for ensuring that training does indeed transfer.

4. Continuing education in the profession must be moved as close to the point of practice as possible.

This is not a fully developed program. It is proposed simply as a means to begin the discussion of what a Green Movement in librarianship might look like and what actions it might take. The intended outcome of such a movement, however, is fully developed. The outcome of such a movement would be the creation of a self-renewing profession. In essence, this movement would advance librarianship from being a learned profession to becoming a learning one.

REFERENCES

1. Peter M. Senge, *The Fifth Discipline: The Art & Practice of the Learning Organization* (New York: Doubleday, 1990), p. 3.
2. Mark Twain, *Life on the Mississippi* (New York: Harper & Brothers Publishers, 1874), p. 57.
3. Ibid., pp. 124-125.
4. *Statement on the Decade of the Librarian 1990-2000* (Chicago: American Library Association, 1991).
5. U.S., National Commission on Libraries and Information Science, *Information 2000: Library and Information Services for the 21st Century* (Washington, D.C.: Government Printing Office, 1991), pp. 3-7.
6. Ibid., 52-53.
7. Strategic Visions Discussion Group, *Vision for Professional Librarians*, 8 December 1991, p. 1.
8. Ibid., p. 2.
9. Timothy W. Sineath, ed., *Library and Information Science Education Statistical Report 1991* (Sarasota, Fla.: ALISE), p. 116.
10. Kathleen M. Heim and William E. Moen, *Occupational Entry: Library and Information Science Student Attitudes, Demographics and Aspirations Survey* (Chicago: American Library Association, 1989), p. 81.
11. Ibid., pp. 82-83.
12. John A. McCrossan, "Public Library Administrators' Opinions of Continuing Education Activities," *Public Libraries* 27, no. 4 (Winter, 1988), p. 48.
13. Ann Thompson, "Special Libraries Association Membership Needs Assessment Survey," *Special Libraries* 83, no. 1 (Winter, 1992), p. 42.
14. Elizabeth A. Stone, *Continuing Library and Information Science Education: Final Report to the National Commission on Libraries and Information Science* (Washington, D.C.: American Society for Information Science, 1974), p. 64.

15. Ibid., pp. 64-65.
16. Ron Blazek and Anna Perrault, "The Role of State Library Consultants in Public Library Reference Work: A Survey," *Public Libraries* 31, no. 1 (January/February 1992), p. 36.
17. Darlene E. Weingand, "Continuing Professional Education," in *Library and Information Science Education Statistical Report 1992*, ed. Timothy W. Sineath (Sarasota, Fla.: forthcoming).
18. Ibid.
19. Mary L. Broad and John W. Newstrom, *Transfer of Training Action Packed Strategies to Ensure High Payoff From Training Investments* (Reading, Mass.: Addison-Wesley Publishing Company, 1992), p. 7.
20. Bruce Joyce and Beverly Showers, "Improving Inservice Training: The Messages of Research," *Educational Leadership* 37, no. 5 (February, 1980), pp. 384-385.
21. *Better Communication = Better Reference Service, A Skill Building Workshop for Library Staff Who Answer Reference Questions-A Trainer's Manual* (Baltimore, Md.: Maryland State Department of Education, 1988), pp. 9-10.
22. Sandy Stephan et. al., "Reference Breakthrough in Maryland," *Public Libraries* 27, no. 4 (Winter, 1988), p. 202.
23. Ibid.
24. Lillie J. Dyson, "Reference Accuracy Survey," *The Crab* (Fall, 1991), p. 7.
25. Ibid.
26. Duncan Smith to Amy Bernath, 21 October 1991 "Preliminary Report of Southeastern CE Providers' Focus Group," School of Library and Information Sciences, North Carolina Central University, Durham, NC.
27. Ibid.
28. Sheila A. Creth, "Staff Development: Where Do We Go From Here?" *Library Administration & Management* 4, no. 3 (Summer, 1990), p. 131.
29. Susan Jurow and Duane Webster, "Promoting Management Excellence in Research Libraries Through Training and Staff Development," *Library Administration & Management* 4, no. 3 (Summer, 1990), p. 143.
30. Sheila S. Intner, "A Field Test of the Library of Congress Training the Trainer Course," *Education for Information* 9, no. 3 (September, 1991), p. 225.

Perceptions of Library Leadership in a Time of Change

Peter V. Deekle
Ann de Klerk

What does the future hold for academic libraries? Are they poised at the brink of an enhanced and integrated role in higher education, or will they suffer the fate of medieval scribes?

A 1991 survey of the chief academic officers and library directors at over 250 small and medium-sized private colleges and universities conducted by the authors of this article showed that there were differences in the perceptions of library futures both among library directors and between them and chief academic officers. While traditional roles were reinforced by many survey respondents, significant innovative expectations of libraries were expressed by several directors and academic leaders. Most respondents acknowledged that changes in library administrative roles are at hand, and a few were prepared to meet the resulting new leadership challenges. It was clear from the survey returns, however, that most directors were awaiting initiatives from their peers before taking action themselves. The survey provided some insight into current perceptions and the authors suggest that the convergence of academic officer and library director perceptions is a starting point for forging a new vision of academic libraries.

The modern academic library has had a tradition of addressing information service concerns independently within the parent institution. Recently, there have been some radical associations with,

---

Peter V. Deekle is University Librarian and Director, Blough-Weis Library, Susquehanna University, Selingsgrove, PA. Ann de Klerk is Director of the Library and Instructional Media Services, Bucknell University, Lewisburg, PA.

© 1992 by The Haworth Press, Inc. All rights reserved.

initially, curriculum development (the Library college, bibliographic instruction, and currently, information literacy) and, more recently, information management (computer-based applications and associated technology, telecommunications, and networking). The influence of these new associations appears to be changing the role of academic libraries and academic library directors, and calls for a closer working relationship with more campus administrative and academic constituencies. Gordon Gee and Patricia Breivik have defined this relationship in the following statement: "Libraries do have a unique role to play in the search for academic excellence-the trouble is, most academic administrators do not know this. They do not plan for or even think about an active educational role for academic librarians."[1] A report in *Research Libraries Group News* further defines this relationship: "Libraries have been able to make a good deal of progress in partnerships with other libraries, but future projects will depend on new kinds of partnerships being forged with provosts, with faculty, with scholarly associations, with campus information czars . . . the shape of the future will depend on these new alliances."[2]

Significant emerging trends in higher education which have major implications for academic libraries include: (1) advances in telecommunications and computer technology, (2) changes in curricula which recognize the interrelationship of academic disciplines, (3) increases in user demand for prompt and responsive information service, (4) a frustrating sense of information overload for both faculty and student clienteles, (5) a corresponding need for greater user discretion and selectivity amid the glut of information, (6) funding and spatial constraints which limit acquisitions, storage, and service options, (7) a need for effective administrative responsiveness toward fundraising and consortial requirements, and (8) the management issues associated with changing organizational structures and staffing in response to changing needs of users.

The authors of this article stated in the cover letter of their survey addressed to library directors and chief academic officers, June 1991, "We believe that the complexity, rapidity and magnitude of the information revolution has contributed to a multiplicity of perceptions about the role of academic libraries in the current teaching/learning process and in higher education in general." The authors wanted to identify what library directors (from now on referred to as "directors") and chief academic officers (henceforth designated "administrators") perceived as the current and future role of libraries and their directors, and the nature of perceptual differences of these two groups.

TOPICS OF CONCERN

This report of survey findings reaches some preliminary conclusions. In a future report, the authors will propose courses of action to help close the perceptual gap revealed by the survey.

Discussions with colleagues in various academic and administrative settings have centered around many of the following topics: (1) Have the responsibilities of librarians really changed? What is the role of library support staff and how does the present library staffing model effectively integrate diverse staff categories? What might be the optimal organizational model? (2) Given the convergence of information and computing technologies, how might the library and computer center most effectively interact and in what organizational structure? (3) To whom does the library report and where should it report? Does the library have a prominent and proactive role in institutional governance structures and in strategic planning institution-wide? (4) What role does or should the library play in curriculum planning and development of information literacy? (5) What role does or should the library play in strengthening the funding base for library and information services? There has been much speculation from many disciplines on the possible effects of the information revolution on libraries and information management, but as yet no clear new paradigm has emerged.

THE SURVEY

The authors decided to seek answers from directors and administrators, since, in common with others, the authors sensed an increased importance of mutual understandings between directors and administrators. Not intending to survey a random sample, an entire population, derived from the Carnegie institutional classifications, was selected. A survey instrument was used to solicit perceptions and ideas on current and perceived trends from the two designated Carnegie institutional groups.

The study of attitudes was based on individual and subjective comments to survey questions; it was not intended to be a statistically controlled study. An initial decision was to send separate but identical questionnaires to be independently completed and returned by directors and administrators from the two clearly defined groups of private colleges and universities, groups in which the authors of the study are currently employed. The survey population included 139 institutions in the Liberal Arts Colleges-Private Colleges I (Survey Group I) and 117 Comprehensive Private Institutions II (Survey Group II). Forty percent of Group I institutions responded, and 35% of Group II. Most responses came from institutions with enrollments of 1,500 to 2,500 students (FTE); half the number of Group I institutions responding to the survey had student enrollments of 1,000 to 1,500 FTE (see Figure 1).

The survey instrument was organized in the five topical sections described above. The authors did not discern major differences among the responses of the two survey groups, directors and administrators of Liberal Arts Colleges I and Comprehensive Universities II. Quotations and references were taken directly from the survey responses without attribution to illustrate, from the authors' viewpoint, a particularly significant perspective on an issue; only the respondent category (chief academic officer or library director) was identified.

Role and Responsibilities of the Library

The first section of survey questions attempted to determine what directors and administrators perceived as the responsibilities of library staff and how libraries were and should be organized to effectively meet those responsibilities. A few respondents saw librarians in a very traditional way: "The primary responsibilities of librarians are to select, make secure, preserve, and provide

FIGURE 1
OVERVIEW OF RESPONSES FROM SURVEYED INSTITUTIONS

LIBERAL ARTS I - PRIVATE COLLEGES

ENROLLMENT	TOTAL SENT	INSTITUTIONS RESPONDED	ANSWERS FROM C.A.O	ANSWERS FROM LIB. DIR.	ANSWERS FROM LIB.DIR & C.A.O	RESPONSES BUT NO REPLIES	NO ANSWER
2,500 - +	14	2	1	1	0	0	12
2,000 - 2,499	20	12	3	10	1	0	8
1,500 - 1,999	26	11	8	9	7	1	15
1,000 - 1,499	50	26	13	18	5	2	24
500 - 999	23	4	2	2	0	0	19
500 or less	6	0	0	0	0	0	6
TOTALS	139	55 (40%)	27 (19%)	40 (29%)	13	3	84 (60%)

Liberal Arts I - Private Colleges = 139

COMPREHENSIVE II - PRIVATE INSTITUTIONS

ENROLLMENT	TOTAL SENT	INSTITUTIONS RESPONDED	ANSWERS FROM C.A.O	ANSWERS FROM LIB. DIR.	ANSWERS FROM LIB.DIR & C.A.O	RESPONSES BUT NO REPLIES	NO ANSWER
2,500 - +	4	2	1	1	0	0	2
2,000 - 2,499	36	16	10	9	3	0	20
1,500 - 1,999	75	23	13	14	4	0	52
1,000 - 1,499	1	0	0	0	0	0	1
500 - 999	1	0	0	0	0	0	0
500 or less	0	0	0	0	0	0	0
TOTALS	117	41 (35%)	24 (21%)	24 (21%)	7	0	76 (65%)

Comprehensive II - Private Institutions = 117
Number of Institutions in 1991 Higher Education Directory = 3,614

access to information sources that are needed by those who use academic libraries." One director wrote, "If librarians are to shed traditional organizational and archival tasks, they are obviously not going to be librarians any more. Why don't we retire the title?" An administrator viewed responsibilities as including: "Organization and direction of the library staff and all policies and procedures regarding budgeting, acquisition, and distribution of library resources."

Most directors and administrators saw the library as having somewhat extended their traditional role quantitatively while not having changed it qualitatively. In the words of one director, "Emerging technologies have already changed some of the operational ways in which we support the curriculum but those changes do not at this time appear to represent a qualitative transformation of a professional mission. Although we are doing it differently, we are still doing the same fundamental things." Another said, "Librarians will continue to serve as the intermediary between information and the user. While how we do it may change, this remains our primary function." An administrator agreed: "The forms of access and the media for information have changed but not the function."

In what ways, precisely, have the library's activities changed? Many respondents acknowledged that libraries still perform the same functions. The survey sought to clarify the nature of libraries' primary responsibilities.

The large majority of both directors and administrators spoke of the importance of educating users: not only collecting or providing access to information sources but also educating library users. Both directors and administrators saw the education function as a high priority. Neither, however, have the successful ways of addressing this priority been specified, nor have libraries advanced as proactive agencies in response to new needs and current pedagogy.

A broader role for libraries and librarians is envisioned by a few respondents. One administrator defined the library's role as "responsive to (even anticipate, if possible) important changes in the delivery of library services; to engage in strategic planning around collections so as to make the best possible use of available resources." Another cited a library's "anticipation and preparation for future need." Still another administrator said that the library's job was to plan "for information services in concert with other administrators."

A director remarked, "Librarians will need to interact with many other campus agencies to a far greater extent then previously." An administrator declared: "It appears the trend will be a concept of the library not as a place, but as a service that can be accessed from many areas. This is a change in philosophy and habit patterns for many."[3]

Discussion

The responses to the survey questions concerning perceived library roles and missions and staffing distinctions indicated a prevailing preference for proactivity. Yet neither directors nor administrators articulated a strategy to ensure or enhance the proactive library. Respondents recognized as appropriate the library's recognized responsibility for increasing information access. The majority desired a larger leadership role for libraries. Only a few responses favored the status quo.

Staffing

The role and position of "highly skilled and educated professionals who are not librarians (often called paraprofessionals) has continued to be an unresolved issue." Several themes regarding this issue have emerged from the comments of directors and administrators. "Certainly, in academe this issue has not been confined to libraries." ". . . It applies across campus as new and rapidly changing technologies continually increase required entry level skills." Several library directors agreed with Larry Hardesty, that "as librarians assume increased administrative, information management and teaching responsibilities, they do indeed shed many of their traditional organizational and archival tasks."[4] They will need to delegate many tasks to others who are skilled and educated.

It was clear that both respondent groups differentiated between librarians and their supporting staff, and other related non-library personnel. There are those positions which have traditionally been called paraprofessionals, that is, support staff with or without bachelor's degrees who have taken on higher level tasks once done by librarians (e.g., many cataloging activities, interlibrary loan, information desk service). There are also an increasing number of personnel who are not librarians but who are professionals in their own right (e.g., systems managers, acquisitions and budget managers with accounting degrees, archivists).

Recognizing the increasing diversity and strengths of library personnel, both library directors and university administrators spoke to the need for staff development support and articulated career paths for those who are professionals but not librarians. Salaries for this group should be reviewed and adjusted to reflect the heightened complexity of job responsibilities. These "non-librarian" staff groups were cited as an integral part of the library team. While librarians should continue to make policy decisions, it was suggested that this group could provide first line supervision and should have input into recommendations. One administrator wrote, "The creation of an exclusionary [sic] caste system based on degree ownership rather than on accomplishment, productivity and competence can be quite harmful."

In regard to librarians, a respondent stated, "The MLS remains the most important single credential for the entry level librarian, but it may not be the only credential for all positions. Increasingly the library staff composed of professionals and paraprofessionals whose education and experience are markedly different from traditional library science backgrounds."

Discussion

As a minimal degree of recognition, it seems to the authors that a term other than paraprofessional must be adopted or devised to recognize important members of the team who now deliver library services. The term should describe what they do in a primary, not subordinate, fashion. The authors note that this issue has long been discussed within the profession and no resolution has been achieved.

The growing complexity and diversity of library staffing was widely recognized by both administrators and directors. The survey returns emphasized the coordination of library staffing activities and responsibilities in a team approach. The authors have associated this coordination of staffing with the library profession's characteristic ability to build partnerships with internal and external agencies and individuals.

Organizational Structure and Inclusion in Governance

The administrative organizational model (in place or preferred) was the overwhelming preference and current prevailing structure in the liberal arts colleges who responded, and a clear but less exclusive preference among responding comprehensive institutions. Although some libraries surveyed were organized on academic lines, they were in the minority and most of the respondents felt this model did not fit the manner in which library services are delivered, requiring as it does a team approach. An administrator pointed out that "the academic model does not work well for those who must work as a team on shared and common goals of service. The flexibility of scheduling and staffing of a teaching department (as well as autonomy of the teacher) are significantly different from the situation in the library." Another administrator succinctly stated: "The library must support the academic program. It is not the academic program. Consequently the organization should be more administrative."

Several respondents talked of a blend or combination as being ideal. Several noted that a collegial spirit could and did prevail in an administrative structure. One administrator said, "Goals are academic, but administrative structure ensures smooth operation." One director commented, "Our hybrid status should be celebrated as a bridge and not bemoaned as some myth of Sisyphus at the mountain of parity with teaching faculty."

The library director reported to the chief academic officer (vice president, provost, dean of the faculty, or a position title which combined these roles) at every responding liberal arts or comprehensive institution, but five. This reporting line was an overwhelming preference among respondents from both groups.

A direct reporting line to the chief academic officer did not ensure a consistent or comparable inclusion of directors in the academic and administrative governance of an institution. Typically, at both liberal arts and comprehensive institutions, librarians were not made part of long range planning groups. One director from a liberal arts college asserted, "The relationship between the director of libraries and the academic officer is critical." Another liberal arts college library director extended this perception: "The missing part of the equation is 'the chemistry' between the president and the librarian."[5]

A director from one comprehensive institution and an administrator from another shared similar concerns about appropriate reporting lines. The director worried that "too many" academic officers already report to one administrator: "The library does not get full [or sufficient] attention." The administrator believed that "the chief academic officer is sometimes too engaged in faculty politics to be the strongest advocate of the library. Only reporting to the president [directly] would help the situation."

One library respondent from a comprehensive institution recognized the lack of inclusion in campus planning groups, but believed that it would be "difficult to argue for a permanent seat on [the] long range planning council because of [the] appearance of preferential treatment compared to other campus needs."

A final perspective on the inclusion of directors in strategic institutional planning and governance was expressed with regret by one administrator from a comprehensive university. The respondent lamented the "lack of analytical and philosophical preparation of most librarians, [precluding their contributions] as full partners in higher education." This sentiment was not overtly stated by other liberal arts or comprehensive institution respondents, but two liberal arts college administrators offered comments which supported the viewpoint. Said one, "I think of libraries as dealing with transient information." The other said that it was appropriate for directors to collaborate regularly with their academic peers in the framework of a "local setting."

Discussion

This section of the survey revealed a nearly universal recognition of the academic library's centrality to the academic program and mission of the institution. Its representation should be at the dean level of academic peers. With most directors and administrators favoring present levels of inclusion in institutional planning and governance, however, a few at each extreme asserted the appropriateness of greater interaction with senior institutional officers, or with less inclusion (due, in part, perhaps, to a perceived lack of broad educational perspective).

The majority of responses from both groups favored the administrative organization model for libraries. The authors, however, recognized that most directors valued a close association with academic programs and their faculty. This traditional association needs, it appears from the survey, to be reinforced and continued, but does not require an academic departmental organization model.

Most directors were frustrated by a pervasive exclusion from strategic institutional planning groups. Some administrators acknowledged the directors' breadth of institutional perspective and experience with program, finance, and personnel management. The authors noted several responses which cited the director's experience in contending with broad and competing constituencies. These views paralleled the observations of Patrick Hill in his 1990 article.[6] The authors are not sure how directors can call attention to their broad view of institutional needs and their expertise in managing large budgets and staffs. The authors suggest that these attributes can be beneficial to both library services and the institution as a whole when they are integrated into the institution's strategic planning process.

Library and Computer Center Relations

Discussion about the optimal library organization model has been going on for many years, but a much newer debate concerns the formal structure for the growing convergence of operations in libraries and computer centers in academe.[7] The survey respondents offered thoughtful suggestions that the concern should be less for compatibility but rather for cooperation and complementary service. Both directors and administrators agreed in theory that these two units were or should be compatible. One director wrote, "I am in charge of both, so obviously I feel they are very compatible.

Management of information services and personnel are [sic] very similar." In general, however, no specific examples of cooperative activities were given and there were many references especially on the part of directors to "turf." There was clear acknowledgement that each unit had different roles to play in the provision of information to the institution. One director described them as follows: the library provides "universal management" for [the] specific needs of clients, the computer center "information storage" for institutional needs. Another director suggested that there was great compatibility in technical applications, but knowledge management was appropriately the library's responsibility. An administrator agreed: "The overlap is mostly technical/mechanical. The primary work of each department is quite different." A recurring theme in the remarks of directors was their sense that computer professionals were not oriented to user service.

Regarding the question of suggested organizational associations between the library and the computer center, the most common recommendation from directors and administrators was that the directors of both should serve on the same planning committees and that they both report to the same academic officer. One administrator felt that the most qualified administrator (librarian or computer center director) should provide overall direction; another said eventually "there would be a single individual in charge of access to information." Another spoke of "shared resources, shared services." At least four library directors were reported as already managing the computer center or academic computing.

There were many suggestions about what skills would be appropriate to both library and computer center personnel. Not surprisingly, many administrators and directors felt that management and interpersonal skills were critical for both groups, as well as technical knowledge and teaching skills. Several directors cited service orientation, common sense, and basic knowledge of what computers can do for the library. In contrast, one director asserted that he was not "convinced that we should try to be DP people in librarians' lab coats. We are book people, purveyors of information, sometimes knowledge, once in a while wisdom, not crunchers of bytes bits. . . ."

Discussion

Computer centers and libraries function, according to respondents, amid an environment of cautious collaboration on the one hand, and guarded territoriality on the other. In view of this, most respondents expressed an interest in improved and closer associations, with each agency reporting to the same administrator. The authors believe that until more clearly defined organizational patterns in academe have been established, administrative oversight of the library and computer operations will likely continue to be based on the perceived competencies and missions (however traditionally defined) of the parties locally involved.

It seems appropriate that the comprehensive scope of library operations and wide range of management responsibilities warrant a serious consideration of directors as principal managers of information delivery, including academic computing. This role is further validated by the library's long-standing expression of a broad institutional vision and service commitment and a long-term identity with an established and international profession. Clearly the relationship between these two important academic services is still being defined in both the eyes of directors and administrators (and surely by colleagues in computing).

Curriculum and User Instruction

Academic libraries during the past thirty years have increasingly moved from a posture of responsive user service toward empowerment of the user through formal orientation and instruction programs. The recognition of this role has increased with the growing need to use technology in teaching.[8] In light of this, the survey questioned administrators and directors concerning their perceptions of the library director's appropriate inclusion in matters pertaining to the planning, development, and review of the undergraduate curricula.

Most respondents interpreted the question as asking solely about the library's formal instruction of its users. Several directors, however, addressed the issue of inclusion in overall curriculum management at their institutions.

Many directors, according to their survey responses, felt a lack of inclusion in curricular matters. This was as strongly prevalent at liberal arts institutions as at comprehensive ones. Most respondents, however, acknowledged that they were involved in the planning and design of courses to the degree that they approved the availability of adequate information resources. One director characterized the librarian's role as "responsive, rather than proactive."

Some administrators recognized the problem of the traditional nature (e.g., user instruction and orientation separated from course content) of library educational involvement. For one respondent from a comprehensive institution, there was an expressed belief that "faculty want more collaboration with the library." This administrator was "unsure how" to accomplish this, and no respondent identified ways to integrate the library into the instructional program.

The perceptions of directors regarding the academic identity of librarians at the departmental level was a related issue. One director from a comprehensive institution regularly taught history courses which emphasized student research skills. This respondent suggested that "the library could play a significant role in designing research courses."

An administrator asserted that librarians, as members of academic departments, were able to teach bibliographic instruction sessions in concert with their faculty peers. Another administrator said that librarians met frequently with academic department chairs on curriculum development matters. A third reported that the director attended any meeting of department chairs where curricular changes were proposed.

While generally supportive, these and other administrators' responses indicated an ambivalence regarding the library leadership role in support of instruction. Indeed, the very informality of many of the cited collaborations suggested to the authors a potential management difficulty in itself.

The concept of bibliographic instruction has included both broad and narrow definitions of library activity. Recently, "information literacy" has offered librarians an opportunity for greater interaction with faculty in the origination and conduct of undergraduate instruction. The survey cited Timothy Weiskel's remark that "there is considerable room here to plan new kinds of strategies to combine training and teaching."[9] A director from a comprehensive institution qualified the prospects for successful information literacy programs, believing that it "must be advocated from the deans and department chairs. If it is seen as a library agenda, it won't get far. It will seem like the library is telling the faculty how to teach."

Directors recognized more readily than administrators the difficulties of establishing and maintaining effective teaching partnerships with faculty. In some cases, lacking a formal voting membership on the curriculum committee, the library director was hampered by the absence of an appropriate forum for participation in academic planning. Despite the opportunities which recent developments in educational technology have brought, some directors believed that "liberal arts college faculty [are] not 'into' state-of-the-art teaching [techniques]." The survey sought to clarify types of librarian/faculty instructional and technical innovations as well as the degree to which libraries perceived their involvement in instructional design and delivery.

Many administrators and library directors reported that the automation of library operations (especially public catalogs) fostered conditions and a supportive climate for further creative instructional collaboration with faculty. From two different comprehensive institutions came these comments: instructional technology will introduce "dynamic conditions with increased opportunities for library contribution" [from a director]; "with the anticipated use of a campus wide communications network, . . . faculty [will] want more collaboration with the library" [from an administrator]. One administrator noted that the computer center already had achieved an "active instructional partnership" with faculty, but not the library. This respondent suggested that "automation of the library invites exploration of instructional role changes [for it]."

Discussion

The library's current involvement in curriculum issues and aspects of the instructional program was largely unsatisfactory to most directors. Several administrators perceived a convergence of information and instructional technology in the audiovisual service agency rather than the library, even where, as is frequent, media services are part of the library organization. The authors suggest that this view can inhibit the provision of a proactive service articulated and anticipated by many administrators and desired by many faculty.

The survey responses supported the authors' contention that instructional media services provide a context in which the library's accepted expertise in understanding user needs, library and computer center initiatives in information technology, and faculty instructional innovations converge. It seems appropriate to the authors that rather than focus on direct student instruction, academic librarians need to promote faculty understanding of information management integrated in the instructional program. On the one hand library directors and librarians need to sit on formal committees to know what is occurring; on the other hand, informal and individual partnerships with faculty will give rise to new ways of assuring information literacy. Building support by the chief academic officers for the library's continued, perhaps new, role in the educational process is critical. Keeping faculty informed about new resources and modes of access is the key to their ownership of library skills and information literacy instruction, in which librarians can play various supporting roles as defined in consultation with individual faculty members.

Fundraising and Development Roles

The final survey section which dealt with the library director's role in developing funding bases was interpreted very differently by individual directors and administrators in both survey groups. It was probably the most misunderstood section in the survey questionnaire. A number of library directors spoke of developing operating budgets, whereas the authors were trying to determine whether directors and administrators anticipated a broader role within the university for the library director in this time of declining financial resources and accelerating costs of information delivery.

The majority of library directors said they had a role in fundraising but with very few exceptions it was limited to working with university relations on the initiative of that unit. Three directors had a very significant role and worked with the president on soliciting donors. A significant minority of the directors responding said they had no active role. Half of the administrators felt the directors had a role, that it probably would not change except that in common with other units there would be more grant writing. One director wrote, "I think the library director's focus should include fundraising in a major way; ideally the library director should be an advocate for the library externally and that his/her expertise should be used to promulgate the library's position in the institution."

Although a few directors felt the development role should increase, it was clear that many directors were apprehensive that a more prominent role would take them away from direct management of the library. Not only did they not want that ("I like being a librarian"), but they felt an associate director would be needed to take care of the internal affairs of the library, and getting an additional staff position would not be possible. By and large neither directors nor administrators wanted the director's role to change. Some interesting comments were made by a very few members of both groups regarding a new role that was perceived to be emerging. Significantly, it was an administrator who remarked, "It [the library] has not been as assertive and aggressive as other parts of the campus but now there is an interest to do so." A director commented, "With the influence of funding sources comes the opportunity to shape the direction of library service and organization." In sum, financial development was a largely passive responsibility for many directors. Administrators tended to articulate a stronger interest in and expectation of library fundraising initiatives.

Discussion

At various points throughout the responses to the questionnaire, there was both implicit and explicit concern about the new things that librarians must now do, and concern that they could not be done along with all the current responsibilities. One administrator wrote, "Inasmuch as libraries are changing very rapidly, a personable and articulate head librarian is more important than ever before in educating prospective donors about the nature and importance of library development." This underscores the findings of one director regarding the importance of a strong personal rapport between the director and the chief academic officer. The authors believe that directors must set priorities for their responsibilities and be willing to give up traditional and probably comfortably familiar tasks, if they are no longer of the highest priority.

SUMMARY

Responses to the broad issue of responsibilities and roles of libraries and library directors revealed a desire for proactivity, yet neither directors nor administrators articulated specific strategies. Coming to grips with changing staffing categories and patterns is an issue which has been debated in libraries longer than many issues raised in this study. How will libraries recognize the importance of professionals and support staff who are not librarians? Can librarians shed some longstanding responsibilities in order to meet the new challenges of the 21st century? The survey responses indicated that many directors are not ready or willing to take these critical steps.

The team approach involving many kinds of personnel was seen to be consistent with the administrative organization model predominantly in place in most libraries; this model was preferred by responding directors and administrators. At the same time a blend of academic and administrative models was seen to characterize library operations: a collegial spirit was considered by many respondents to be important. Almost all directors reported to the chief academic officer (known by varying titles). Directors were disappointed in their lack of inclusion in high level strategic planning. Administrators generally did not perceive this inclusion as significant.

A more recent issue is the convergence of library and computer center roles and functions. While there was general agreement in the compatibility and complementary relation of libraries and computer centers, concern over "turf" was a recurring comment from directors. The prevailing view among all respondents was that both units should report to the same academic officer, and that their directors should serve on some of the same governance groups.

Information literacy and the library's involvement in curricular matters were unfamiliar concepts (and many respondents misinterpreted the meaning of "information literacy"). More than one administrator saw the locus of converging technologies embodied by instructional media services, without acknowledging its being an accepted and integral component of existing library services. The authors urge, therefore, the promotion by the library of faculty understanding of information management.

Fundraising was the least understood and appreciated survey topic. While library directors would theoretically like a proactive role rather than being reactive to development office initiatives, they were more concerned about diversion from direct internal library management functions.

CONCLUSIONS

Survey responses revealed an acute awareness among library directors that libraries and librarianship are changing. Administrators are aware of new trends in information management, but, perhaps not surprisingly, are not as acutely aware as directors. Except for a few directors, specific approaches to changes were not suggested. Many directors would like a stronger role in institutional planning and more recognition for the role of the library in this regard. The authors discerned, however, considerable apprehension on the part of many that limited staffing and perceived roles precluded some directors from focusing attention outside the library. Sometimes this was based on the desire to continue to be a librarian "in the traditional sense."

Administrators in general did not recognize directors' qualifications for broader administrative participation. They did not perceive librarians as possessing extensive experience with multiple institutional constituencies and in partnerships with other libraries and consortia. Perhaps because of the library's historical tradition as the "heart of the university," faculty and administrators have not perceived the recent transformations in library activities and roles.[10]

Computer operations seem to have captured greater faculty and administrative attention and interest. Ernest Boyer illustrated the tendency to take the library's presence for granted in the following remarks: "One college we visited described the library as 'the focal point of learning on the campus.' And yet, despite the idealism expressed in this statement, we found the library . . . to be a neglected resource."[11] If the institution lacked a library, faculty and students would be concerned, but, considering Boyer's observations and the survey responses, the authors believe that many academic libraries can be conveniently ignored, like many predetermined institutional fixtures.

The survey demonstrated that, concerning the library's role and mission, there is a considerable gap between the perceptions of academic administrators and directors. Similar to the collaborative efforts of RLG libraries, library directors and administrators of private liberal arts and comprehensive institutions might collectively define a more comprehensive role. The authors also suggest workshops for faculty to promote a shared ownership with the library of information literacy.

The authors are convinced that a new approach to the support of a library's teaching function is warranted, one which would allow the integration of information services, computer technology, and instructional media services. To succeed, this new approach will need to include a more comprehensive role for directors on the strategic planning levels of this integration of functions.

The survey revealed that many library directors were concerned about taking a broader information service role. The authors believe, however, that library leaders can appropriately-and indeed must-provide the vision for the integration of information resources, information structures, and scholarship, resulting in overall knowledge management. If, as one of the respondents said, "Computer technology is instrumentality rather than an end in itself," then libraries, with vast information delivery experience and a history of faculty collaboration, as well as strong service traditions, are capable and worthy of leadership.

As some of the respondents suggested, we believe that there is a need for library directors (1) to become more politically aware, (2) to improve their management skills through education and appropriate training, and (3) to develop stronger working relationships with both faculty and academic officers. In the words of one director, "We need visionaries who seek to develop a new and mutually supportive future without bias and without having feet mired in the past . . . without capricious discarding of the past."

NOTES

1. Patricia Senn Breivik and E. Gordon Gee, *Information Literacy: Revolution in the Library* (New York: Macmillan, 1989).
2. "RLG Sponsors Series of Provost-Librarian Meetings," *Research Libraries Group News* 25 (Spring 1991), 12.
3. Pat Molholt, "Libraries and Campus Information," *Academic Computing* (February 1990), 20-21.
4. Larry Hardesty, "The Bottomless Pit Revisted," *College and Research Libraries* 52, no. 1 (January 1991): 3-4.
5. See also Hardesty, *ibid*.
6. Patrick Hill, "Who Will Lead the Reform of Higher Education? Libraries, Of Course!," *Washington Center News* 5, no. 2, 1-16.
7. Peter Lyman, "Computing, Libraries and Classrooms," in *Organizing and Managing Information Resources on Campus*, Brian L. Hawkins (McKinney, Texas: EDUCOM, Academic Computing Publications, Inc., 1989): pp. 207-227.
8. Thomas Kirk, "Teaching and Technology: The Impact of Unlimited Information Access on Classroom Teaching," *Library Issues*, 9, no. 6: 1-4.
9. Timothy Weiskel, "The Electronic Library: Changing the Character of Research," *Change* (November-December 1988): 38-47.
10. See Ann de Klerk, "Heart of the University, Empty Phrase or Resource for Teaching and Learning," *Talking about Teaching* (Lewisburg, PA: Bucknell University, 1988).
11. Ernest Boyer, *College, The Undergraduate Experience in America* (New York: Harper and Row, 1987).

Library Assistants in the Year 2000

A. Ann Dyckman

Library assistants are already a crucial component of libraries. However, they are often overlooked, underpaid, and unappreciated, and a steady supply of replacements is taken for granted. As technology drives the field of information management, the importance of a highly trained, dedicated staff will continue to grow. Yet demographic changes in the American workforce will make such employees difficult to recruit and a challenge to retain. At the same time, major changes in our society will revolutionize the way institutions do business.

This article will focus on factors that will affect the relationship between libraries and library assistants by the year 2000, and the resulting changes in libraries' organizational structure, policies and procedures, and the compensation structure.

TRENDS AFFECTING THE GENERAL WORK FORCE

According to the Bureau of Labor Statistics, the composition of the work force in 2000 will be a little over 52% male and 47% female. Three-fifths of all women over age 16 will have jobs. Blacks, Asians, American Indian, Pacific and Alaskan Native workers will fill 16% of the positions. Non-caucasians will make up 29% of new job holders between now and 2000. Increasing numbers of immigrants will enter the labor force.

However, this rise in the number of women, minorities, and immigrants will not be the only change affecting the work force.

A. Ann Dyckman is the Director of Personnel, Cornell University Library, Ithaca, NY.

© 1992 by The Haworth Press, Inc. All rights reserved.

Other trends may be equally significant. For instance, by the year 2020, one out of three people will be age 50 or older. By the year 2000, the average age of employees will be 39 and this will increase to 41 by the year 2020. Robert Goddard notes that "The present aging population is the most educated, most bureaucratically, organizationally and politically sophisticated federation of older people ever. With those skills and experience, great amounts of discretionary time and strong personal incentives, they are likely to become a potential political force inside and outside organizations."[2]

Along with this aging and increased sophistication of the population goes a reduction in the pool of young workers entering the labor force. A growing number of this younger group do not have either technical skills or post high school education. Applicant pools will be older, more diversified, and those interested in entry level positions will have less skill and education. Those applicants who do have the skills and education will demand and get high pay. So employers will work harder to retain skilled workers.

This better educated, older, more diverse work force will demand a better balance of work and family/leisure time. The high number of dual career workers will have the financial security to make more demands from their employers. "The new value shift centers among time, quality, self-fulfillment, children, and general satisfaction with life. Americans are increasingly assertive of their rights in and out of the workplace."[3]

TRENDS AFFECTING CORPORATIONS AND INSTITUTIONS

Changes Resulting from Technological Advances

"The technologies of telecommunications and computers are revolutionizing the structure, management and productivity of the work force" warns Robert Goddard in "Work Force 2000."[4] Already, almost half of all employees are information workers and by 2000 the number will have increased substantially. "Because technology now is shifting corporate priorities from where you stand in the hierarchy to what you know, the manager of the future will be less a decision maker and more a moderator of a collegial process."[5]

Most jobs are already demanding higher skill levels and more education, and by the year 2000, a majority of all new jobs will require post-secondary education. This " . . . increasing importance of education and skill also will revise the social structure of organizations. Task forces will be organized around problem solving by groups of relative strangers representing a diverse set of professional skills. These groups will evolve in response to a problem rather than programmed role expectations . . . Rank and status won't count as much as flexibility and functionality according to education, skill and professional training."[6] There is a trend toward participatory management with a blurring of the roles of managers and staff. Employees are finding themselves reporting to two bosses: the project manager and the functional manager.

Economic and Political Factors

Due to the needs generated by high tech workplaces, employers may turn to paying for the work rather than the time of employees. Traditionally, employees have been paid for hours of work usually in a well defined location. The fluid nature of technical problems often requires the use of project groups, with members chosen for specific skills. This need may dictate a new approach to employee compensation, paying for output not input, and " . . . the result of this (will be) a new organizational structure: temporary and part-time workers overlapping a new lean bureaucracy."[7]

American firms must now compete in a global market and many are emphasizing service in order to survive. "It no longer matters how much employees produce; what matters is how good the products and services are and how closely they meet individual customer needs. Because information and knowledge are the vital raw materials of the products and services produced, and the creativity, innovation and application of these two elements are contributed by individuals and groups, the modern worker must be recruited, organized, managed, trained and regarded much differently than his or her industrial predecessor."[8] Ruth Bramson emphasizes the importance of employee attitudes, stating "Employee attitudes have a critical effect on the success of any service program. A group of people who are burned out, turned off, cynical or demoralized, or who suffer from any combination of these problems can simply fail to buy into the spirit of any service effort. The support, or at least the readiness, of the people in the organization is vital . . . There must be optimism, motivation and energy in employee attitudes."[9]

Women will gain more political and economic power. Since they will make up a majority of the pool of qualified applicants they will have far greater choice of occupations. As a result, they will demand more appropriate compensation, especially in fields traditionally dominated by women. Women currently make up 93% of single households, and receive only 69% of the pay that men receive.

Government Action

Federal regulation is expected to increase, especially in the area of benefits, as is the number of conservative decisions by the Supreme Court. The cost of benefits will continue to rise, resulting in a continuation of the trend to share the cost with employees. There will be an increase in the flexibility of benefits, especially those related to dependent care. Although the rise in the number of female workers (many of whom are single parents) has already begun, most organizations now have benefits and working regulations that have been designed for a male workforce that is not responsible for dependent care. These patterns will change, as employers seek to retain skilled workers.

Modifications will be necessary in legislation affecting hourly workers. The Fair Labor Standard Act has not been changed since the thirties, and is woefully out of date with the needs of today's workers. As more workers work in locations other than the traditional office or factory settings, and are paid for the task not the time, the Act will grow even less useful. Also, given the growing complexity of jobs, and the need for creativity and problem solving, defining "professional work" is increasingly difficult. Regulations surrounding mealtime breaks can hinder instead of help flextime workers.

Changes in the Work Climate

Environmental and safety issues will receive increased attention including the safety of equipment and chemicals in the workplace and attention to substance abuse.

The workweek will be shorter, and employees will be able to take advantage of more opportunities for flex-time, job-sharing, and other adjustment that will help meet the needs of the growing number of female workers.

Transportation issues will grow in importance as congestion grows, especially in urban areas that are not large enough to support good mass transportation systems.

PRESENT PRACTICES AND TRENDS IN LIBRARIES

Libraries will be strongly affected by many of the changes noted above. The demographic change in the applicant pool will mean that the ready pool of bright, educated young women that libraries have depended on for a large percentage of their employees, will have many other opportunities. Already libraries are losing a steady stream of technically trained employees to higher paying jobs outside the library. Retention of these employees will require that salaries, work policies and benefits better meet the needs of female workers.

The Growing Emphasis on Service

Although libraries are nonprofit organizations, they must compete for operating funds, either through fund raising, or by convincing parent institutions or municipalities of their needs. Due to the increasing complexity of methods to access information, quality of service will become as important as the quality of the collections in attracting adequate support. Libraries have traditionally been noted for service, and one of the remarkable features of a large number of these institutions is the loyalty and dedication of their staff, both librarians and library assistants. However, a combination of factors including low pay, low morale, more responsibility without increased compensation or status, and the availability of other opportunities is causing dissention. An angry rumble is rising, especially among library assistants.

Technological Changes

Technological changes have and will continue to have profound effects on libraries, influencing even their basic organization structures. Just like other organizations, libraries are experiencing the need for project or working groups, selected for the complementary skills of the individual members. As team members, individual contributions are valued and encouraged, and the traditional pyramid structure of authority changes into a circle, with information flowing in and out. As more and more jobs grow dependent on the use of computers, creative ways of cross-training and diversifying responsibilities becomes critical to avoid physical problems caused by too many hours in front of terminals and burnout caused by repetition.

The Shift of Responsibilities from Librarians to Paraprofessionals

The explosion of information and methods to access information has modified the mission of libraries, and therefore changed the structure. According to Jennifer Cargill, "Libraries and librarians will remain the guardians of information; methods of accessing the information will continue to diversify" and, "As more routine tasks are eliminated through shared databases, through the benefits of technology, and through delegation to support staff, librarians are freed for managerial responsibilities, coordination of staff, and assignments requiring special training or subject emphasis." [10]

Numerous articles in library journals document a growing shift of responsibility from librarians to library assistants. Paul Dumont wrote in 1989 that the "role of the library technician in technical services has changed radically, requiring a more knowledgeable, computer-literate worker with greater skills and adaptability." [11] Patricia Eskoz compared surveys of catalog librarians in 1983-84 and 1986-87 and found indications of a gradual shift of more complex cataloging to support staff, especially in larger libraries.[12] Reporting on a survey of job responsibilities and job satisfaction at the University of California Libraries in the 1990 issue of *College and Research Libraries,* Patricia Kreitz and Annegret Ogden found that even activities traditionally reserved for librarians, original cataloging and name authority control, were now just as often the responsibility of library assistants. In conclusion, these authors reported that " . . . our study has found a major overlap of responsibilities in the area of creating bibliographic access, small but provocative overlaps in the areas of collection development and public services, and a strong division of responsibilities in management-related activities."[13] Larry Oberg in his article "Paraprofessionals: Shaping the New Reality" in the May/June 1991 issue of *MOSAICS,* mentions several factors that are causing tasks to shift from librarians to support staff: technological changes, budget constraints, and the increased participation by librarians in research, governance, teaching and research. He warns that the resulting blurring of roles between librarians and support staff is angering library assistants who feel they perform the same work for less money and status. He also feels this role-blurring is causing an acute identity crisis for the profession.[14] Library assistants in the Cornell University Library are now performing tasks that were formerly performed by librarians in almost every area of the library, including original cataloging, interlibrary loan, collection development, and reference. Yet at the present time, these employees are not well paid, they have little status in the system, and in some instances their work is not even considered "exempt."

Professional Affiliation

At Cornell as in other libraries, there is a rise of a "middle class" of paraprofessional staff who are articulating their needs. The number of exempt, non-librarian positions in the Library rose from 7 out of 284 in 1981 to 57 out of 337 in 1991. Although a good portion of these were in areas such as computing, development, and administrative services, 56% of the 1991 group were "library family" positions. As this group grows in libraries, there is a congruent growing recognition by the library profession of the value of increased participation by paraprofessionals in national associations. The American Library Association Council approved the formation of the Membership Initiative Group on Library Support Staff Functions, and the group held its first meetings during the 1991 ALA Midwinter meetings, in Chicago. An ACRL Task Force chaired by Sheila Creth, University of Iowa, has recommended steps to increase the involvement of paraprofessionals in association activities.[15] Another indicator of this trend to focus on the interests of library assistants at the national level is the new journal *MOSAICS* and the increase in the number of articles devoted to related topics in other national journals. The profession is waking up to two equally vital sets of needs: the needs of paraprofessionals in terms of recognition through compensation and status; and the growing need for these employees by librarians.

The Battle for Appropriate Classification Levels

Libraries are requiring more and more training and education in general/subject education, computer related skills, expertise in library techniques such as bibliographic searching, and management and supervisory skills for many of their library assistant positions. This is one factor eliciting a glimmer of recognition of the high level of responsibility in these positions by parent organizations, such as universities. Library personnel staff are realizing the need to capture the true responsibility of library assistants in language that can be understood outside the library. Joseph Coates captures the elusive complexity required by many new technical jobs saying, "A characteristic of many of these new critical skills is the ability to interpret as well as absorb information, which requires more systematic and abstract knowledge."[16] A task force of librarians at Cornell spent two years writing a generic list of library tasks to provide guidelines to supervisors preparing job descriptions. The tasks, grouped by function area, were listed in increasing levels of difficulty. The Task Lists were also designed to help in the current classification review at Cornell, and indeed have been very helpful. (The outcome of the review is still pending, but indications are positive.) Many library assistants in other academic libraries are also undergoing classification reviews. The result of these reviews can hinge on how effectively the job descriptions convey the complexities of many tasks performed by the staff. Lucy Cohen, University of Michigan, in her article describing the new classification system for technical and supervisory library assistants at her institution, reported that . . . "it became very clear that the most important part of this study was to describe the work being performed at the Library to University Personnel staff members and to educate them about the complexities of library tasks and the breadth of responsibilities inherent in technical and supervisory positions."[17]

FUTURE CHANGES FOR SURVIVAL

Libraries, like other institutions, will change many practices and policies related to human resources in order to survive. Some of the most striking changes will be those affecting library assistants.

Recruitment

Competition for applicants with appropriate skills will change recruitment in libraries by demanding a proactive approach that involves marketing strategies. Librarians must deal effectively with the invisibility of the field, and this will take a concentrated effort at the national level. Pay scales will rise, both to attract and retain. Serious consideration will be given to groups of people now ignored or at best tolerated such as the retired, persons with disabilities, immigrants and members of minority groups. Two new case studies discussed in "Studies refute myths about older workers" in the July 1991 issue of the *Society for Human Resource Management* found that "older workers can be trained at new technologies, are flexible about work assignments and schedules, have lower turnover and absenteeism than their younger colleagues and are often better sales people."[18] Older workers will become valued for their experience, skills, and wisdom.

The organizational climate will change, so that different is not so often perceived as less desirable. In order to attract and retain a more diverse population of employees, other workers will be sensitized to the importance of judging by performance, not by physical characteristics.

Strategies for Retention

Retention of skilled workers will become one of the most important goals of institutions in the next decade. The cost of replacement will rise dramatically, both in loss of work time due to the difficulty of finding good replacements and in the training of new staff. This is the area where libraries must change substantially. At present, many libraries provide an entry level training ground, losing skilled employees to an increasing number of higher paying jobs requiring similar training. This familiar cycle of constant training and high attrition will become cost prohibitive.

In order to retain library assistants, two serious problems must be reversed to increase morale: low status with little recognition for their contributions and low pay. The role that librarians play in this change will be critical.

A Rise in Status and Pay for Library Personnel

The librarians of the future, especially those who keep up with technology and can contribute to their institutions through management skills, will be paid well, and will have the status that will leave them unthreatened by highly skilled paraprofessionals. In fact, the existence of these paraprofessionals will be recognized as essential to the librarians, allowing them to have the time and energy to handle increasingly complex technological and managerial issues.

The term "professional" will not be used to distinguish librarians, since it implies that other library workers are non-professional. This designation is now very damaging to employees' self esteem and morale. Other professions such as medicine and law do not distinguish categories of employees with the term "professionals," excluding other personnel such as medical technicians, paralegal assistants, and nurse practitioners.

Library assistants may have ranks, determined by the individuals' skills and experience rather than classification levels, based on a set job description. "The person, not the job, may become the most important element in determining work parameters, authority, responsibility and salary grade, the real and potential value of the tasks assigned, and so forth."[19] Many libraries use this system now for librarians, and a similar system for library assistants will provide much more flexibility and help with the perception of many long-term staff that "there is no place to go." Expanding job challenges through such methods as cross training, quality circles, increased participation in decisions, and job rotations will become common practice. These practices will also help alleviate problems caused by sitting too many hours in front of computers.

A Movement Toward Flexible Working Conditions and Benefits Structured for Individual Needs

Responding to a more vocal, political set of employees, employment practices will be modified to better fit the diverse needs of employees, from persons with disabilities to single parents. Libraries will offer more flexibility in benefits and hours worked, offering flextime, job sharing, dependent care leaves, etc., to attract and retain employees. Growing transportation problems will dictate creative solutions, allowing more employees to work at home, or in cluster locations.

The Modification of the Organization of Library Personnel

The structure of libraries will change to incorporate a more fluid work force with project teams and task forces concentrating on targeted problems. According to Robert Goddard, "One of the strongest changes underway is toward increasing individual and small group independence and self-reliance. The concept connotes a complete reversal of the fundamental notion that everyone works for someone else. Instead, it says employees work only for themselves, that they take responsibility for their performance, progress, and futures, and that they have the knowledge and the capabilities necessary for success .... Managers and employers must design procedures to help identify, employ, and motivate and reward these individuals and teams, and to recognize and support self-reliance. It means a power loss for those at the top who design, manage and control the day-to-day activities of others."[20] Library supervisors and managers today are often overworked, and harried as they struggle to carry too much of the burden. As the workload continues to grow this uneven carrying of the load must be shared if the managers are to survive. All employees in the future will carry more organizational responsibility by sharing in the planning and implementation of goals. By becoming a part of the planning, they will commit more readily to the goals and therefore more effectively contribute to the implementation. The responsibility for running a library, even a small department is already in many cases too complex and time consuming to rest on one or two managers.

An Increase in Training and Professional Development

The library profession will accept the growing necessity for systematic training and professional development of all staff. This will mean a recognition that resources must be shared rather than the present practice in many libraries of supporting the professional development only of librarians. Ways of providing increased opportunities for continuing education and professional growth for all staff must be found despite the cost in dollars and work time. Given scarce resources, this change will demand creative solutions. Regional meetings will increase in importance, with shared accommodations, rides, etc., helping cut costs. Libraries will use more in-house talent to train, requiring staff who attend outside workshops to bring back the information and help train others. Opportunities for new methods of group communication will develop with innovations in the field of fiber optics.

CONCLUSION

Libraries are already and will continue to be strongly affected by demographic changes affecting the general work force and trends affecting corporations and institutions. An aging, politically astute, diversified work force will be employed for higher pay and fewer hours in positions requiring ever higher levels of skills and education. The organizations will be formed of matrixes, with less hierarchy. Employees will be compensated for work accomplished, not hours spent.

Libraries which survive to the year 2000 will be challenging, exciting, and enjoyable places to work for both library assistants and librarians. However, critical changes must occur in the conception of the organization. How libraries are organized and the role of all employees must change to keep up with the demands of technology of the demographics of the work force. Robert Goddard captures the essence of some of these changes saying, "It requires an idea about work that the employees are the organization and they have the intelligence, wit and desire to use their knowledge for the goals of the organization. It also suggests that employees' loyalty and enthusiasm are not required, contracted or automatic, but earned. Increasing the dynamism of the work force; providing for the needs of working families with children; bringing women, minorities and immigrants into the work force; improving the education and skills of employees, adapting to new technology; and forging a new social contract with workers are not the only items on the nation's agenda between now and the year 2000. But they certainly are among the most important."[21] In the article "Future Trends in Public Library Administration," Maurice Marchant and Mark England conclude that " . . . if improving service is more important to them (libraries), they will use participative alternatives to create humane working environments where innovation can drive good planning towards high performance. Over the long haul, the transition to a participative approach that fits the pattern of a modern information system will be required for the library to survive and flourish . . . libraries today must develop patterns of behavior that will accommodate change, and, to the extent possible, lead future developments rather than just react to them."[22]

The warnings are clear and the time is short. Ten years is not a very long time to make such radical changes.

REFERENCES

1. Library Assistants is only one of many terms used to denote library employees who are not librarians. I have chosen this one because I feel it has less negative implications than other more common terms such as non-professional or support staff.
2. Robert A. Goddard, "Workforce 2000," *Personnel Journal* 68:65-71 (Feb. 1989).
3. Joseph F. Coates and others, "Workplace Management 2000," *Personnel Administrator* 34:51-55 (Dec. 1989).
4. Goddard, "Workforce 2000," p. 67.
5. Ibid., p. 69.
6. Ibid., p. 70.
7. Ibid., p. 69.
8. Ibid., p. 70.
9. Ruth N. Bramson, "The Secret Weapon in the War for Customers," *HR Magazine* 36, no. 1:65 (Jan. 1991).
10. Jennifer Cargill, "Integrating Public and Technical Services Staffs to Implement the New Mission of Libraries," *Journal of Library Administration* 10, no. 4:21-31 (1989).
11. Paul E. Dumont, "Creativity, Innovation, and Entrepreneurship in Technical Services," *Journal of Library Administration* 10, no. 2/3:63 (1989).
12. Patricia A. Eskoz, "The Catalog Librarian–Change or Status Quo? Results of a Survey of Academic Libraries," *Library Resources and Technical Services* 34:380-392 (1990).
13. Patricia A. Kreitz and Annegret Ogden, "Job Responsibilities and Job Satisfaction at the University of California Libraries," *College & Research Libraries* 51:297-312 (July 1990).
14. Larry R. Oberg, "Paraprofessionals: Shaping the New Reality," *Library Mosaics* 2,5:11-12 (May/June 1991).
15. "ACRL Task Force Recommends Increased Paraprofessional Participation," *Library Mosaics* 2,4:6, (March/April 1991).
16. Joseph F. Coates, "Workplace Management 2000," p. 53.
17. Lucy R. Cohen, "Creating a New Classification System for Technical and Supervisory Library Support Staff (At the University of Michigan)," *Journal of Library Administration* 10, no. 4:59-85 (1989).
18. Society for Human Resource Management, "Studies Refute Myths About Older Workers," *HRNews*, July 1991, p. 8.
19. Goddard, "Workforce 2000," p. 70.
20. Ibid., p. 70.
21. Ibid., p. 71.
22. Maurice P. Marchant and Mark M. England, "Future Trends in Public Administration," *Journal of Library Administration* 11, 1/2: 1-22 (1989).

Recognition of the Role of the Librarian: Position Classification at Yale

Jack A. Siggins

At a time when academic librarians are increasingly concerned about their status on campus, their changing roles in the academic community, and appropriate recognition for their contributions to the success of the university, the place of librarians in position classification structures has become a focus of increasing attention. Librarians have watched in despair as university officials at their institutions not only fail to acknowledge the importance of their contributions, but also sometimes decline even to involve them in deliberations directly affecting their classifications and salaries.

In February 1989 Yale University announced that a comprehensive study of Yale's managerial and professional job classification and salary administration programs would be undertaken. Hewitt Associates, a nationally known consulting firm, was hired to work with Department of Human Resources staff and others to develop a new job evaluation system and address a broad range of other issues, including salary equity, market competitiveness, and the special needs of the growing professional staff.

President Benno Schmidt, in a letter to each Management and Professional (M & P) staff member, explained that the study was also in response to expressions of concern from the staff about classification equity and career growth opportunities. The system in place then was based on a nine-grade classification structure that

---

Jack A. Siggins was formerly Deputy University Librarian at Yale University, New Haven, CT.

© 1992 by The Haworth Press, Inc. All rights reserved.

had been implemented in 1976. In the intervening years, major changes had taken place both within and outside the University in skill requirements, work patterns and career opportunities. The number of M & P staff had increased from approximately 900 to over 2,400, while the number of separate positions had grown to more than 300.

The M & P staff comprise the third group of permanent employees at Yale, along with faculty and clerical and technical staff (C & T). Faculty include all tenure and non-tenure track teaching positions; C & T's include both exempt and non-exempt positions, most of which are covered under contracts with either of the two labor unions at Yale, Locals 34 and 35. Librarians are included in the M & P category, along with positions in administration, athletics (including coaches), clinics, communications, computing, development, dining halls, facilities, finance, human resources, museums, research, safety, and student services.

Excluded from the M & P category and from the study were non-faculty administrative positions (e.g., assistant deans) and all medical doctors. Also excluded from the study was the category of staff designated the "Executive" group. These positions included the most senior positions which reported directly to officers of the University (the officers include the President, Provost, Vice-Presidents, and Deans of Yale College and the schools). For instance, the University Librarian, who reports to the Provost, was included in the Executive group. In addition, however, certain other senior positions were made part of this group, such as the Deputy University Librarian position, which was included because of its high level of responsibility and the fact that it reported to a position which functions at the level of academic dean.

Concurrent with President Schmidt's letter, the Associate Vice-President for Human Resources informed deans, department heads, and directors of large administrative units of the project. His letter outlined the major steps to be followed in the process, including the development of a questionnaire to be completed by all managerial and professional staff describing the duties and responsibilities of their respective positions and asking for the assistance of each administrator in making the project successful. Meetings were subsequently held with several of these administrators to provide further explanation and to seek their guidance.

A central element in the project was the establishment of a committee comprised of M & P staff members who would be given the task of reviewing all the questionnaires and developing a new classification structure. Nominees were solicited from senior administrators of departments across campus, and in June 1989, eleven persons were appointed to the Management and Professional Job Evaluation Committee. Although the Committee members were selected from ten different administrative units, they were not chosen to represent the interests of their respective areas, but instead were selected to represent all M & P staff with specific qualifications in mind: experience at and understanding of the University; knowledge of M & P jobs; objectivity and analytical skills; credibility among their peers; and the ability to work within a group. The senior administrator among the appointees, the Deputy University Librarian, was named Chair of the Committee.[1]

In early June 1989 questionnaires were sent to all M & P staff. For the next several months, attention was focused on gathering the completed questionnaires. The staff of Human Resources provided additional instructions, guided department heads through the process, and encouraged staff through regular written communications to complete the questionnaires as expeditiously as possible. Despite these efforts and a series of deadlines for submitting the questionnaires, the response from M & P's was below what was considered by Hewitt Associates and Human Resources to be an acceptable rate of return.

Discussions with staff and administrators revealed that the causes of the delay seemed to arise from three conditions. First, some of the department and unit administrators resisted the project or did not take it seriously, with the result that their staff members felt no urgency or need to respond. To overcome this, the importance of cooperation was emphasized to the department heads by senior university administrators. Second, there were numerous misunderstandings about how to fill out the questionnaires and the information that should be included in them. This condition was resolved satisfactorily by intensifying the number of meetings and training sessions conducted for staff by Human Resources specialists and by a series of articles in two Department of Human Resources publications.

The third level of resistance was the result of a pervasive mood of skepticism among many staff about the purpose and need for completing the questionnaires. Some staff doubted that anything positive would evolve from their effort, a feeling based in part upon the inequity that had evolved over the years within the old classification and salary structures. Others pointed to the failure in the past of Human Resources to maintain the integrity of the classification system in the face of pressure from some faculty to give special treatment to or make exceptions for the M & P staff working for these faculty. These latter attitudes were more difficult to overcome. A strategy was devised in response to this resistance which included meetings of Human Resources staff with heads of key administrative units at which they were encouraged to apply pressure on their staff, without making completion of the questionnaire a requirement. Human Resources also provided regular reports to the administrative heads on the number and percentages of submitted questionnaires in their units and throughout the University.

It was made very clear that all jobs would be classified, whether a questionnaire was submitted or not, using job descriptions if necessary. Many unresponsive staff then realized that a review of their position would be more accurate if based upon a questionnaire they themselves had completed. Eventually, completed questionnaires were received from more than 72% of the M & P staff.

The Committee began its work by receiving comprehensive training in job evaluation theory and practice from the staff of Hewitt Associates at their offices in Rowayton, Connecticut, and on campus. In January 1990, the Committee met with the Vice-President for Administration and Finance and the Associate Vice-President for Human Resources to clarify the Committee's tasks. Out of these discussions came a written charge to the Committee and a mission statement. The mission statement declared simply: "By development of a new Management and Professional position classification structure, enhance the University's competitive ability to attract and retain highly competent staff and offer career path alternatives." The Vice-President's charge to the Committee stated that the Committee should: (1) develop a hierarchy of all managerial and professional positions by evaluating jobs according to compensable factors; (2) communicate the Committee's process and progress to M & P staff; (3) consult with the Department of Human Resources and Hewitt Associates on the development of a compensation system, including initially such issues as the number and structure of salary grades, salary ranges, job audits of individual jobs, an appeals process, and a mechanism for continual evaluation of the classification process; and (4) submit a report of the completion of the above to the Associate Vice-President for Human Resources at the earliest possible date, but no later than September 1, 1990.

At the end of January 1990, the Committee began the task of reading the questionnaires and developing a new position classification structure for the entire M & P staff. To do so required careful preparation before meeting all day each Tuesday until the task was completed in the Winter of 1990.

PROCESS

Of the four primary tasks assigned to the Committee, the most time-consuming was that of development of a hierarchy of managerial and professional positions. The method selected by the University administration and Hewitt Associates called for comparing and categorizing content and then ranking all positions to attain classification equity. These rankings would then be used for salary administration purposes by Human Resources and Hewitt. To do this analysis in as objective a manner as possible, a factor comparison approach was selected. The ranking of positions in the University would be determined by taking factors (position characteristics or specifications) inherent to a greater or lesser extent in every position and comparing them, one factor at a time, with the same factor in every other position. This analysis, comparison, and ranking was done for every position, except those of the Committee members themselves, which were ranked separately by Hewitt Associates (not by the Human Resources Department). The position rankings by each factor then combined to form a composite or overall ranking which established a complete position hierarchy.

Five factors were identified by University officers as the critical elements of M & P work for purposes of comparison and ranking. These were: Knowledge and Skill; Problem-Solving and Decision-

Making; Scope and Complexity; Impact and Accountability; and Internal/External contacts.[2] All five factors were considered to be of equal value; that is, none was weighted to have more importance than the others.

The primary sources of information for the analysis process were the questionnaires submitted by the M & P staff. Several other sources, however, also contributed vital information. Foremost among these were presentations by heads of major administrative departments or functions. In all, thirty-four individuals from eighteen administrative areas met separately and privately with the Committee. They included deans, directors, and vice-presidents with responsibilities for: athletics, clinics, communications, data processing, development, dining halls, editing, facilities management, facilities planning, finance, human resources, law, libraries, museums, research, safety, auxiliary services, and student services.

These senior administrators participated in two ways. First, each was invited to make an oral presentation to the Committee and to submit any explanatory documentation. The purposes of these presentations were to provide an overview of each unit's activities, to describe the relationships and functions of each position, and to convey the administrator's view of the comparative significance of each position relative to the overall mission of the unit. Prior to each presentation, the administrator was provided a thorough explanation of each of the five evaluative factors and was asked to make his or her comments at least in part in the context of those definitions. Second, after the Committee had arrived at a preliminary ranking for a major unit, the administrator of each unit was asked to review the rankings for his or her area and offer comments as a way to clarify the perceptions of the Committee members and resolve serious misunderstandings. Each administrator's comments were noted and considered by the full Committee during its final deliberations.

Another source of information was the knowledge of the Committee members themselves. Their experience from working directly or indirectly with a wide range of persons across campus provided valuable information and insight which greatly assisted the Committee in understanding the work of many positions. The range of working experience at Yale among members of the Committee ranged from eight to twenty-five years. Several of them had worked in more than one administrative unit during their careers at Yale. Each of them included budgets among their present responsibilities; several also had personnel functions among their duties. All Committee members had advanced degrees, including one with a Ph.D. In addition to their knowledge and experience, however, the most important characteristics each brought to the process were the ability to be objective, a commitment to the success of the project, and the ability to participate effectively in a group decision-making process.

Recent position descriptions were a fourth source of information about certain positions. They were used, however, only when questionnaires were unavailable. The final source was additional data provided by M & P staff in informational meetings held in various departments and in two general meetings. These meetings were organized by members of the Committee with assistance from Human Resources staff. While the primary purposes of these meetings was to allow Committee members to inform M & P staff of the Committee's progress, explain the process, and answer questions, several M & P's took advantage of these occasions to point out facts about their individual positions and the work of their units which they felt the Committee might overlook or misinterpret.

The Committee adopted certain ground rules for reviewing the questionnaires:

1. Base the evaluations on those requirements, responsibilities, and conditions of the position which are a regular part of the assigned position.
2. Evaluate the position as described in the questionnaire and not as it was in the past or might be in the future.
3. Consider only the position's requirements, not the merit of the individual filling the position.
4. Do not allow the title of the position to influence the evaluation, since titles do not always accurately describe the actual responsibility of work performed.
5. Have all the questionnaires read by one or more committee members; at least 80% of the questionnaires were read by all Committee members.

6. Do not let knowledge of the job market–that is, the pressure to pay higher salaries for certain positions due to outside competition for qualified staff–influence relative rankings.
7. Avoid allowing personal bias, prejudices, or pre-conceived ideas about where a job should be ranked to color judgments.

Positions were organized and reviewed by "family," or type, of job; for instance, financial positions across the campus were reviewed together. Several positions within each family were selected as internal reference points, or "benchmarks," which were later used to make comparisons among job families easier, to help develop the classification structure, and to enable Human Resources and Hewitt Associates to compare Yale's salaries with those of outside competitors for like jobs. In all, more than 100 benchmark positions were selected.

While Committee members worked toward developing a position hierarchy and classification structure, they also identified and discussed several specific issues and concerns, such as the development of a structure which is more responsive to the needs of professionals among the M & P staff. In this exercise, the presentations made to the Committee by senior managers of the various administrative units were particularly valuable. The Committee organized and presented its thoughts on these matters to Human Resources for further study and action. Several of these suggestions were presented in the recommendations section of the Committee's final report (see below).

RESULTS OF THE STUDY

The Committee fulfilled its charge. A hierarchy of M & P positions was completed and submitted to the Associate Vice-President for Human Resources, along with a new grade structure for the fifteen job families. The number of salary grades was increased from nine to twelve in order both to accommodate reporting structures within individual units and to maintain the integrity of the total job hierarchy system. In addition, the number of position titles was reduced from 300 ranked plus 302 unranked jobs to 250 ranked jobs. Some titles were changed to make their relationship to similar positions more apparent and to identify career paths more readily. The Committee submitted the twelve-grade salary structure it had developed to Human Resources and Hewitt Associates, who then developed a salary structure which the Committee reviewed.

OTHER RECOMMENDATIONS ARISING FROM THE STUDY

As the Committee proceeded toward its goal, several issues outside the scope of its charge but of importance to the success of the University's objectives evolved out of the natural flow of discussion and analysis. The Committee identified several matters related to the classification system which would have great impact on the success of both its implementation and acceptance by the M & P staff. These were discussed in advance with the Associate Vice-President for Human Resources and his staff in order that there would be no surprises for them, and so that the implications of the Committee's suggestions could be studied thoroughly. In all, ten issues and suggestions were forwarded, of which the five described below were accepted and implemented as part of the new structure.

1. Career Paths

The Committee identified natural sequences of appointments which both professional and management staff might seek as part of a career path leading to promotions and positions of greater responsibility. These sequences supported the University administration's stated desire to retain Yale's capable staff by offering them opportunities to develop skills and make additional contributions.

2. Classification Decision Appeals

In order to give staff a way to appeal M & P classification decisions made by the Department of Human Resources, a review panel was established with authority to make a final determination. This panel is comprised entirely of senior M & P staff, including initially some members selected from the M & P Job Evaluation Committee. New members are to be trained in the five factor comparison system used in this study.

3. Review of M & P Classification System

A mechanism for the systematic and ongoing review of the M & P classification system will be developed to ensure that the system continues to be responsive to job skill requirements and other changes.

4. M & P Description Format

Several changes in the position description format used by Human Resources have been made. The new format now incorporates the five compensable factors employed by the Committee in its study. In the months following the implementation of the new system in April 1991, all M & P position descriptions have been re-written, thus assuring at least initially greater uniformity, consistency, and equity in describing the hundreds of positions across campus.

5. Introduction of the New Classification System to M & P Staff

The Department of Human Resources and the Committee jointly prepared and carried out a plan for the introduction of the new system to the M & P staff and the campus generally. This included, first of all, a series of explanatory documents delivered to all administrative heads of departments and to each of the 2,400 M & P staff. It was followed immediately by a series of meetings conducted by the Department of Human Resources with the participation of members of the Committee. Individual Committee members also organized explanatory meetings with staff in each of the departments with whom they had been in contact throughout the process, as well as any others who made a special request for a separate meeting.

OTHER RESULTS OF IMPLEMENTATION

A thorough discussion of the impact of the changes brought about by this program cannot be discussed comprehensively in this article; indeed, many of the effects will not be revealed for some time to come. Some of the more immediate and important ones, in addition to those already mentioned, are summarized below.

Salary Adjustments

At one of its meetings with the Vice-President and Associate Vice-President at the beginning of the project, the Committee members raised the issue of whether and to what extent the University would provide funds to pay for salary adjustments which would be required as a natural result of classification adjustments for some positions. As experienced administrators and managers, each Committee member felt a degree of skepticism about how the University would pay for the adjustments, especially if the burden of funding were to come from the budgets of the administrative units themselves. The Committee was assured that the units would not have to pay for the increases out of their own budgets, and that funding had been set aside to cover the cost. True to their word, the officers of the University provided funding for all the adjustments beginning on the first day of implementation, April 1, 1991. This was followed on July 1 by the normal annual salary increases. In all, 55% of the 2,400 M & P staff received a special adjustment, ranging from as little as .1% to as much as 15%, depending upon where they stood in the new ranking compared to the old. The University decided also that every person who qualified for an increase would receive a minimum of $250, even if salary calculations under the new ranking system would call for a smaller amount.

Market Competitiveness

One important result has been to make Yale more competitive in attracting and retaining persons with important skills. As the result of extensive surveys of salaries in the Northeast, Hewitt Associates made salary recommendations both for the general salary ranges and for specific jobs for which qualified candidates were in short supply. The result is that for the next few years at least Yale will be better positioned to compete for talented individuals.

Credibility of University Policies

The thoroughness and openness with which the project was conducted convinced most of the M & P's that the results were equitable. They saw clear evidence that the University administration appreciated their contribution. Staff and managers also became more knowledgeable about job ranking and salary scales and therefore more skilled in defining and describing their positions.

Credibility of Human Resources

With a fair system in place and firm support from both the Yale community at large and University officers, the Department of Human Resources should now be better able to maintain an equitable classification and salary system, and to resist pressure from some faculty and administrators who may demand exceptions to the system to accommodate particular members of their staff. The burden no longer falls solely on Human Resources to justify a denial of a reclassification or salary adjustment; it now is up to the administrator to provide arguments sufficient to convince not only Human Resources but also ultimately a committee of M & P peers.

IMPACT ON THE LIBRARIANS

As positive as the results of this project were for other M & P's, they were even more so for librarians. Librarians benefitted in three areas: classification changes, salary adjustments, and recognition in the Yale community.

Among M & P's at Yale, librarians comprise the second largest sub-category (the Medical School is the administrative unit with the largest number of M & P's). Librarians are one of the "families" into which all M & P's were placed for purposes of evaluation.

Some library positions, however, were reviewed as part of other families; for instance, positions in the business office, security, museums (conservation/preservation), personnel, systems, and editorial projects were evaluated in those respective groups.

The remainder were also part of an internal library ranking system which had been in place for almost twenty years. Each of the five librarian levels (Librarians I through V) had a comparable M & P salary grade assigned by the Department of Human Resources. In the old system of nine M & P grades, the five librarian ranks ranged between the second lowest and the second highest M & P grades, with the Associate University Librarians unranked. Under the new system, the five ranks ranged between the fourth lowest and the third highest, with the AUL's in the second highest grade (see Table 1, below). These shifts created an advance in grade in relationship to other M & P's.

TABLE 1

Old System		New System	
M/P Grade	Librarian Rank	M/P Grade	Librarian Rank
Unranked		31	
		30	AUL
		29	V
10		28	
9	V	27	IV
8		26	
7	IV	25	III
6	III	24	II
5		23	I
4	II	22	
3	I	21	
2		20	

Although the Librarian I-V series had comparable M & P rankings in the old Yale classification system, minimum salaries in the two structures did not correspond. For instance, the entry level Librarian I rank had a minimum salary almost $2,400 more than its equivalent M & P salary grade. This disparity also occurred in the other four librarian ranks. In fact, the minimum salaries for Librarians I, IV, and V (comparable to M & P salary grades 3, 7, and 9, respectively) were more than the minimums for M & P grades 4, 8, and 10, respectively. The Department of Human Resources had resisted efforts to raise the M & P grades for librarians in order to bring them in line with the librarian salary minimums, arguing that the classification ranking was appropriate in relationship to the work performed in other M & P positions around the campus. For more than twelve years, fortunately, the Provost had responded positively to the University Librarian's argument that the librarians' salaries needed to be higher in order to compete more effectively for talented staff. The contradiction prevalent in this situation was typical of the inequity and inconsistency which permeated the old classification system. The new structure brought the librarians' salaries in line with those of the M & P grades, thus removing a source of great confusion.

As a result of their higher placement in the M & P grades, many more librarians received salary adjustments in April: whereas 55% of all M & P's across campus gained increases, 83% of the librarians received them. In addition to many pleased librarians, these increases place Yale's librarian salaries at a much more competitive level nationally. For instance, the Association of Research Libraries' salary survey figures for Fiscal 1991 ranked Yale 17th nationally among beginning professional salaries. Taking into account normal increases at other institutions, Yale should jump to approximately 5th position when salary figures for FY 1992 are released. Comparable improvements in median and average salary rankings are expected.

As significant as these improvements in classification and salaries are, the most remarkable gain for librarians from the project has been that the work librarians perform is very highly regarded on campus. This is a feeling held by both their fellow professionals and members of the University administration.

The message was conveyed in two ways: first, through the very high ranking of librarians in the new classification system; and second, by the fact that two librarians were appointed to the Job Evaluation Committee itself by the University administration, and one of them was named to lead the process by serving as Chair of the Committee. Throughout the hundreds of hours of discussion, members of the Committee other than the two librarians repeatedly placed higher value on library work than on other types, such as development, research, nursing, safety, athletics, and museum curators. Later, when this phenomenon was reported to them, most librarians at Yale were pleased, but not surprised. They are confident of how important their work is to the intellectual vitality of the campus. The message contained in this project was an affirmation of what they have known for a long time.

Given a similar opportunity to compare job factors, librarians, administrators, and faculty at other universities might also become aware of the same fact.

NOTES

1. To illustrate the diversity of backgrounds of the Committee, their titles and departments are listed here:
    Senior Financial Analyst, Capital Management
    Manager, Compensation and Classification, Human Resources
    Director, Academic Computing Services
    Business Manager, Pharmacology, School of Medicine
    Director, Administrative Affairs, Faculty of Arts and Sciences
    Manager, Administrative Services, Development and Alumni Affairs
    Deputy University Librarian, Library
    Head, Library Personnel Services, Library
    Associate Director, Finance and Administration, Athletics
    Business Manager, Facilities Management
    Administrator, Therapeutic Radiology, School of Medicine

2. Although the Committee was provided with more detailed definitions of the five factors, they can be summarized in the following way:

KNOWLEDGE AND SKILL
    The knowledge and skill necessary to achieve the results required by the job. This factor focuses on the level or depth, as well as the variety, of knowledge and skill required by the position.

PROBLEM-SOLVING AND DECISION-MAKING

The degree to which judgment, analysis, and creativity must be used in planning and investigating problems and evaluating alterative solutions. This factor considers the degree and latitude allowed in making decisions, as well as the variety, type, and frequency of decision-making.

SCOPE AND COMPLEXITY

The independence of action, level of work involved, and the nature of supervision exercised by the position. Consideration is given to the planning and organizing required by the position in terms of complexity of objectives and goals to be accomplished. Consideration is also given to the direction received and supervision exercised.

IMPACT AND ACCOUNTABILITY

The accountability involved in achieving the results required of the position: whether it is primary, shared or indirect accountability. Consideration is given to the impact that actions and decisions have on the University, the amount of risk taken, and the general level of importance of the decisions made.

INTERNAL AND EXTERNAL CONTACTS

The nature, significance, and frequency of interpersonal/human relations skills required by the position, exclusive of direct interaction with staff supervised or superiors.

The Rhetoric of Performance Management: A Training Problem and Two Solutions

George Soete

The evidence is all around us that individual performance management, in the form of performance goals and goal-based self-assessment, is ever more widely acknowledged to be a key tool in library management. The surge of recent interest in strategic planning has placed new emphasis on the development of organizational goals and goal-based evaluation systems. The quality management movement has shifted the emphasis away from some of the more rigid aspects of management-by-objectives (e.g., quotas) toward the view that goals and goal-based self-assessment are a creative and flexible means of continual quality improvement. And the shift toward self-managing work groups and other highly participatory models in some of our libraries has suggested a strong need for individual and small-unit performance planning through the use of goals and objectives: if work groups and the individuals in them are to manage themselves effectively, they need the tools to do so.

While they typically acknowledge the importance of such performance planning, organizations are nonetheless faced with significant problems of training and orientation when they decide to require performance objectives and meaningful self-assessment of staff. This article describes what one academic research library, the University of California at San Diego (UCSD), is doing to train staff in performance management skills.

George Soete is Associate University Librarian at the University of California, San Diego, CA.

© 1992 by The Haworth Press, Inc. All rights reserved.

BACKGROUND

Until the late 1980's, goals and objectives had been only an informal part of the performance review process for librarians at UCSD. Though self-reviews of librarians occasionally mentioned goals and objectives, in reality they were often ignored as part of the process. Moreover, written self-reviews, a key part of the review package, typically took the form of unevaluated lists of activities rather than carefully assessed accomplishments that were explicitly related to organizational goals.

Three developments within the last few years have led to an intensification of the goal-based self-evaluation process throughout the library:

1. A new University Librarian stipulated that performance reviews for librarians be goal-based and that statements of goals become a formal part of the evaluation process. Goals and objectives, formerly discussed on an informal basis between supervisor and librarian, were now to be part of the official review file as well. An important parallel expectation was that goal-based reviews would be truly evaluative—in their self-reviews, reviewees were expected to focus on measurable accomplishments, on the value of those accomplishments to the Library and its users, and on both the strengths and areas needing improvement in their performances. Though these may seem innocuous changes on their face, the implications for accountability were significant, and so a generous period of transition to the new system was provided.
2. The Library developed a comprehensive Strategic Plan, *The Library Without Walls*, with a hierarchy of mission, goals, objectives, and action plans. The clear message was that departments and individual staff were to look to the Strategic Plan for guidance in developing their own goals and objectives, which would further the goals of the Plan.
3. Through a change in University personnel policy, non-librarian professionals (for example, technical and management staff in the Systems Office, the Library Business Office, and processing departments) were required to develop goals and

objectives each year and to relate annual performance evaluations to goals.

Suddenly, like it or not, some ninety professional staff, both librarians and non-librarians, were responsible for developing performance goals and objectives, relating them to the goals of the Library and their departments, and measuring their performance against those goals.

As with any significant organizational change, some anxiety resulted and a number of concerns were expressed. There was concern that goals which were perfectly reasonable at the beginning of the year might be superseded by goals related to new program development, the need to work on urgent projects such as journal cancellations, or any one of the myriad problems that one simply cannot plan for in a large, dynamic organization. Staff wondered if there would be penalties if all performance goals were not achieved. What about the ongoing aspects of performance–daily service at a reference desk, original cataloging, materials selection? Wouldn't it be difficult to construct goals for these "routine" activities that were an everyday part of one's core job? On a more practical level, some staff were simply less comfortable than others with the rhetorical challenges–the *writing* tasks–represented by the new expectations, especially the potential discomfort of suggesting in a formal written document that there might be areas for self-improvement.

The burden of interpreting these changes and training staff in related new skills fell on the supervisors, who had always been–and remain–key actors in the performance review "partnership." To help both supervisors and reviewees with these important new tasks, the Library has developed two training tools: a half-day workshop in goals and objectives and a model goal-based self-review that suggests but does not impose a framework for the process.

The workshop developed out of a request from librarians that training in the goals and objectives piece of the process was needed. Late in 1990, Susan Jurow of the Office of Management Services, Association of Research Libraries, after several consultation sessions with Library Administration, offered a day-and-a-half workshop for all UCSD librarians, including administrators. In 1991, the author conducted three follow-up events for staff who had not attended the 1990 workshop: (1) a brief session for librarians early in the year; (2) a five-hour workshop for non-librarian professionals around the same time; (3) a joint half-day workshop for both librarians and non-librarian professionals during the fall. It is the latter workshop, adapted from the original Jurow design, that has become the continuing annual training event for new professionals. It is offered each fall just before performance reviews begin.

As a parallel training effort, even before the workshops were offered, the author had developed a fictitious goal-based self-review to illustrate what he had in mind when he thought about such a document. Though originally intended only for those in his reporting line, this model has been made available to most other professionals in the Library.

These training efforts were meant to achieve several purposes:

1. to demystify the performance goal-setting and self evaluation processes;
2. to promote the view that planning with goals and objectives could enhance individual performance effectiveness;
3. to relate the performance goals process to organizational goals and organizational effectiveness;
4. to save professionals time as they perform this annual task.

THE WORKSHOP

The workshop is scheduled to run from 10:00 a.m. to 3:30 p.m., with an hour for lunch. It is held on campus but away from the library to intensify focus on the task at hand. After a review of the objectives of the workshop and the agenda for the day, participants are asked to consider three key questions:

1. What is a goal?
2. What do you like/value about the goals process?
3. What do you dislike about the process?

The resulting census is reported on flip chart sheets. This exercise, especially the like/dislike section, gets issues and problems out for discussion as soon as possible, enabling participants to articulate both positive and negative feelings while at the same time having their responses become merged in the total group response.

Next, a conceptual framework for performance planning is provided. *Planning* is a classic managerial responsibility; developing goals and objectives is, furthermore, a key activity in planning. The organizational context is presented: the Strategic Plan, the goal focus of Library planning, and the requirements of the performance review process for all library professionals.

The benefits of goals and objectives in an organizational setting are then enumerated:

1. Goals clarify where we want to go so that we understand better how to get there.
2. They decode expectations for all to see and understand;
3. They establish a foundation on which to build improvement;
4. They help us coordinate our activities with other departments, staff;
5. They help us distribute work and effort more equitably.

Next, goals and objectives are related to *performance measures*, a key concept in the remainder of the training. Four types of measures commonly applied to staff performance are described:

1. EFFORT, which describes *inputs* (example: 43 person/hours of planning time);
2. PROCESS, which describes *activities carried out* (example: three meetings, one conference call, and a final report);
3. PERFORMANCE, which describes the *results of effort* (example: on line search service established);
4. OUTCOMES, which describe *final effects* (example: better service to users).

Effort and *process* are often used as measures of performance because they are easiest to capture. *Performance* and *outcomes* are more difficult to measure and are thus often slighted in the goal-setting and self-evaluation process, but they are, in fact, more indicative of actual useful accomplishment. In constructing performance goals, though all kinds of measurable goals are possible and even useful, the most useful are those that point us toward *performance* and *outcomes*. Throughout the rest of the training, participants are pushed to develop goals that can be measured in these ways.

The focus on measurable results provides the framework for the next exercise. Here the participants gain some practice in converting "raw" work activity into measurable results. A few examples are offered to get them started on a group exercise:

Activity	Measurable Results
1. Fundraising	a. number of dollars raised b. number of contacts made with potential donors c. improved grant-writing skill as measured by peer judgement
2. Working the reference desk	a. number of questions answered successfully b. improved reference interview skills as measured by user satisfaction survey

Participants are then given a chance to work together in small groups practicing the shift from work activity to measurable result. Their work is reviewed and discussed by the entire group.

Now the group is ready to work on goals and objectives. First, three basic kinds of performance goals are enumerated:

1. *Organizational Goals.* These directly further the work of the organization. Examples: to develop a new service for library users; to improve an existing service; to change a processing procedure to improve both efficiency and accuracy.
2. *Performance Effectiveness Goals.* These are instrumental goals related to the manner in which staff carry out their work. Such goals might relate to: time management, delega-

tion, communication effectiveness, ability to plan and organize, training skills, effective relations with colleagues.
3. *Professional Goals.* These describe how the employee intends to make a contribution to his or her profession, as appropriate, through such means as presentation and publication.

Next, the criteria for effective performance goals are reviewed:

1. Goals should suggest *movement* from a present state to a desired state; use of words such as *enhance, improve, further,* and *increase* denote such movement.
2. They should be *measurable,* preferably in quantitative terms. Some goals are best stated in qualitative terms: even these can be measured, for example, by seeking feedback through surveys and comments from other staff.
3. They should, whenever possible, *reflect organizational goals* and should clearly be seen as advancing its mission.
4. They should be *challenging but achievable.* When one sets too many goals or unachievable goals, frustration results.
5. They should be *ranked in importance* if possible. Part of performance planning is determining priorities.
6. They should be *dynamic and adaptable to change,* especially if circumstances change significantly. Target dates should be included, if possible, as an aid to setting priorities and allocating time.
7. They should be *reviewed and renegotiated regularly.* Such an approach provides both a periodic check on progress and a safety valve in case a goal turns out to be impossible to achieve.
8. They should be *focused.* A key question for the staff member is, what are you working on in your performance? A focused goal-based plan might include: (a) two or three major projects, (b) development of one or two new skills or knowledge areas, and (c) work on one or two performance dimensions (example: time management). It is not necessary to develop goals to cover every area of one's position description–such an approach can in fact lead to a feeling of being overwhelmed and frustrated.

9. They should, if possible, indicate an *ultimate aim*. In a service organization like an academic research library, such an aim would, of course, be service.

Participants are then given an opportunity to convert the material already generated (job activities and measurable results) into goals and objectives. This work is also done in small groups. Problems and issues arising in this exercise are discussed in the larger group.

The final exercise of the afternoon is a "goals clinic." Participants are asked to provide the trainer ahead of time with some of their previously written goals and objectives; they are asked particularly to submit goals that they have had problems writing. The trainer rewrites these slightly to protect anonymity, but the basic form is left intact. The entire group then gets a chance to critique these "masked" goals, using the principles learned through the experiences of the previous few hours. Participants are thus engaged in the process of creating specific, measurable goals at several junctures throughout the workshop.

THE MODEL SELF-REVIEW: LUIS LIBROS

The other training device used is a written model–a fictitious self-review by a librarian named Luis Libros, who works at a fictitious UC campus. The model is intended not only to illustrate effective performance goals and objectives but also what a performance review based on those goals and objectives might look like as well. Three performance review issues are illustrated: (1) that the self-review focus on *accomplishments*; (2) that it be truly *evaluative*, not merely descriptive and enumerative; and (3) that *both strengths and areas to work* on in the performance be cited. Here is an excerpt from this self-review:

* * * *

Goal #1. Improve my skills in mediated on-line searching.

Objective: Attend tutorial on new [psychology] database to be offered on campus, 1990.

Objective: Take on a larger share of departmental searching load; increase load by 50% to 15 searches per week by January 1991.

Accomplishments: As a relatively new librarian in the Ed/Psych Library, I needed to enhance basic skills. I was comfortable searching only 9 databases at the beginning of the period, and per session searching time was too long. The tutorial turned out to be a marketing strategy by the publisher, but it did serve to outline the basic structure of the database, which I have searched several times since. Doing more searches was a useful approach–a powerful motivator for me. I have been doing 13-16 searches per week.

Evaluation of accomplishments: On-line time has decreased by 28% on the average, and my "scores" on user evaluation forms have gone from an average of 7.1 to an average of 9.2. I can now search 22 data bases with ease and 15 others with occasional references to the manuals.

Areas to work on: For the time being, my department head and I are satisfied with my progress and believe that more practice is the key to further enhancement of skills and greater user satisfaction.

Goal #2. Enhance contribution to the orientation/instruction program for new graduate students in Education.

Objective: Redesign two-hour orientation session by June 1990 so that newly designed sessions can be offered September 1990.

Objective: Develop one-hour sessions on ERIC, PSYCH-LIT, and DISSABS for new masters students by October 1991.

Objective: Develop twelve special screens on Curriculum Collection for hypercard orientation installation by February 1990.

Accomplishments: The two-hour orientation session redesign was completed and new sessions offered as planned. Only the ERIC session was developed and tested. It was found that most students do not attend structured sessions on searching end-user databases, so we focused on point-of-use instruction instead. Responsibility for the hypercard screens was given to another librarian.

Evaluation of accomplishments: Pre- and post-testing of students indicate preliminarily that the two-hour orientation sessions are more effective than our previous three-hour sessions in communicating basic information about the library. I have gathered from site interviews that the point-of-use handbook I developed on PSYCHLIT has been very popular and effective in helping students get the most out of their searching. I am working on a similar handbook for ERIC. I had more enthusiasm than skill for the hypercard project and am glad that my department head suggested it be reassigned.

Areas to work on: Instructional design is an area of strength for me, and I would like to make it even stronger by taking two relevant courses in the School of Education during the next review period. At the same time, the hypercard experience taught me that I need to acquire basic skills in the use of computers in teaching and reduce my apprehension about it as well.

* * * *

All of the training objectives for the model self-review are illustrated in this excerpt. The objectives are specific and measurable. The focus is on results and outcomes rather than on effort and process. Accomplishments are really evaluated and areas to work on are candidly appraised. Though the outline is very structured, it allows a certain flexibility, even informality, of expression. In presenting the model to the staff, we have encouraged them to use it or not, as they choose, but the expectation remains that the key elements of specificity, measurability, focus on accomplishments, and true evaluation of both strengths and areas to work on be present.

EVALUATION OF RESULTS

Though no formal evaluation of these training tools has taken place, anecdotal reports of improvement in the quality of self-reviews and the goals and objectives on which they are based suggest some positive results. Of course, the benefits of supervisorial attention to these new expectations and the fact that reviewees have now gained more practice are significant factors as well. Nonetheless, informal comments solicited in preparation of this article suggest some direct benefits of the training. Many participants found the first day-and-a-half workshop useful not only for its content but also because the presence of administrators, participating throughout the event, enabled the group to address issues of organizational culture. About this and the later workshops, participants responded:

1. that such an approach promotes shared values and brings consistency of practice throughout the library;
2. that talking about the problems, the issues, and the writing tasks with colleagues–knowing co-workers have the same anxieties–made the process go easier; some participants have continued the process of helping one another with goal formulation;
3. that the workshops presented direct clarification of administrative expectations;
4. that it was helpful to learn that there was more than one way to write effective goals and self-evaluations;
5. that it was useful to receive criticism through the anonymous process of the goals clinic.

Many respondents have found the model self-review useful as well, particularly those engaging in the process for the first time.

1. Again, the model clarified administrative expectations.
2. Even though the format was not always followed exactly, the model provided a clear guide to required ingredients in the self-review and useful suggestions about tone and approach, especially in evaluative sections.
3. Supervisors have found it useful in helping to explain their expectations in the review process.

Finally, some respondents gave clear credit to their supervisors in helping them through the process, with one person citing "the more useful [but also] more painful iterative process of working with my supervisor to define goals and objectives and to make reviews reflect them."

CONCLUSION

The UCSD experience suggests that taking a training approach to performance management can make a difference in improving the quality of the goal-based self-review process and thus the effectiveness and relevance of organizational planning. Such an approach focuses on the most fundamental behavioral level-the writing skills needed to develop effective performance goals, objectives, and self-reviews-rather than on the more theoretical aspects of the subject. The integration of librarians and professionals who are not librarians in the training, even though their needs are somewhat different, proved successful. Most importantly, this training approach rests on the assumption that individual goal-setting and self-evaluation represent an important direction for our organizations if we are to capitalize on the creativity that results when staff are empowered to manage themselves within a framework of clearly articulated organizational expectations.

BIBLIOGRAPHY

King, Patricia. *Performance Planning & Appraisal: A How-To Book for Managers*. New York: McGraw-Hill Book Company, 1989.

Olson, Richard F. *Performance Appraisal: A Guide to Greater Productivity*. New York: John Wiley & Sons, 1981.

Stueart, Robert D. and Maureen Sullivan. *Performance Analysis and Appraisal: A How-To-Do-It Manual for Librarians*. New York: Neal-Schuman Publishers, 1991.